"There is a power behind his words found only in the most celebrated of spiritual teachers. By living from the depths of this Greater Reality, Eckhart clears an energetic pathway for others to join him." — Russell E. DiCarlo

Author of *Towards a New World View: Conversations at the Leading Edge*

"Fresh, revealing, current, new inspiration. Out of the many spiritual books that cross my desk this one stands out from the flock. . . . If you are considering getting back in touch with your soul, this book is a great companion."

— Joseph Roberts, *Common Ground,* Vancouver, British Columbia

"I have no hesitation in recommending Eckhart Tolle's wonderful book. Everyone I know who has picked up a copy has ended up taking it home. *The Power of Now* sells on its own merit and by word of mouth."

— Stephen Gawtry, Manager, Watkins Books Ltd., London

"*The Power of Now* was introduced to me by a customer. I read only one page and agreed that it rang true. It is a jewel of clarity and insight. The book has become a word-of-mouth bestseller here at East West."

— Norman Snitkin, Co-manager, East West Bookshop of Seattle

"*The Power of Now* appeared at Banyen's with almost no publicity, and immediately became a bestseller. This seems to be the 'right book' for many people at this point in time. The writing is clear as a bell; the words ring true. Truly an exceptional book that promises to make a real difference in people's lives."

— Tom Oakley, Banyen Books, Vancouver, British Columbia

THE POWER OF
NOW

THE POWER OF

A GUIDE TO SPIRITUAL ENLIGHTENMENT

Eckhart Tolle

Yogi Impressions
MUMBAI, INDIA

Yogi Impressions

Yogi Impressions Books Pvt. Ltd.
61, Anjali, Minoo Desai Road, Colaba,
Mumbai 400 005, India.
Website: www.yogiimpressions.com

Copyright © 2001 by Eckhart Tolle

Book and cover design: Jacqueline Verkley
Photographs of Author:
Back cover: Colin Low
Inside: Mutribo

Originally published in Canada by
Namaste Publishing Inc., 1997
and in the United States by
New World Library, 1999

First India printing: March 2001
Seventh reprint: September 2002
ISBN 81-901059-1-4

Printed at: Thomson Press, New Delhi

You are here to enable the divine
purpose of the universe to unfold.
That is how important you are!

— Eckhart Tolle

CONTENTS

PUBLISHER'S PREFACE

I had the good fortune of attending Eckhart's retreat at Hollyhock on Cortes Island, just outside Vancouver, Canada, in September 2000. About 120 people from various parts of the globe converged there, after reading the book which you now hold in your hands. The book impacted them so much, they traversed many miles across continents just to listen to and be in the presence of this great spiritual teacher.

If I were to sum up the essence of Eckhart's teaching in one phrase, it would be 'Present Moment Awareness'. This is the core of 'The Power of Now', and this is what you feel deep within yourself, in his presence. He shows us the way to focus on the present, instead of living in the past or worrying about the future — a state of consciousness, free of the burden of time. As Eckhart puts it: "Nothing ever happened in the past; it happened in the *Now*. Nothing will ever happen in the future; it will happen in the *Now*."

In this book Eckhart uses a simple question and answer format, to reveal to us our true nature. It makes the book simple to read and easy to comprehend. The book is best read perhaps a few pages a day, to enable one to reflect upon the words, and experience the truth of what has been read. Eckhart holds your hand like a guardian angel, and takes you step-by-step towards leading a life free of suffering and angst. It explains how we create our own pain and constantly make the mistake of identifying with our minds, thinking *that* is who we are. And the true beauty lies in grasping a new meaning each time you read the answer to a particular question or life situation.

The magical quality of this book is that Eckhart uses words to take us to a place beyond words, where silence resides. And in this silence, this inner stillness, we access the *Now*. In this *Now*, the Present Moment, problems do not exist, for the *Now* is all there is.

Indeed, silence has been recognized as the key to the spiritual dimension, perhaps with different words, by Masters of many traditions — and in particular Indian philosophy — no doubt a reflection of the timeless value of this wisdom. In the words of Ramesh S. Balsekar, a well-known contemporary Master of Advaita: "The whole point is that the potency of silence lies in the very interval between thoughts, which is precisely what is being sought, the reality of the whole-mind, the absence of conceptualizing. In other words, this metaphysical silence is precisely what is being sought (by the spiritual seeker): the 'Buddha-mind' of the Chinese Ch'an, the 'Witness' of Advaita, the 'Father' of Christianity... Thus, all that is needed is for the perpetual movement of thought to be arrested, for us to be awakened."

Eckhart is like a breath of fresh air, as he is not aligned to any particular teaching or guru. And what is truly remarkable is how he has touched so many lives with the first book he has written. Its message is universal in appeal. Since it was first published in Canada, 'The Power of Now' has sold hundreds of thousands of copies, and has been translated into 20 languages. I have personally met many people who claim this book has transformed their lives, as well as their relationship with themselves and others. It is my sincere hope this book does the same for you.

What is truly fascinating is how blessed we are to receive this book at the turn of the millennium, as humanity enters a higher level of consciousness. There is an upsurge in the number of people on the spiritual path who seek to improve the quality of their lives, and who are striving to make the world a better place. We are all indeed spiritual, and this book helps us realize the same. In Eckhart's own words, "I cannot tell you any spiritual truth that deep within, you don't know already. All I can do is remind you of what you have forgotten."

On the last day of the retreat, as we were busy packing our bags to leave, Eckhart's parting words were, "Remember, you're not going anywhere. All things come and go. But you are not what happens. You are the silent space in which all things happen." And that is what 'The Power of Now' is about. It's the truth spelt out — the truth about life as it is — Now! It's more than just a book. It's a companion for a lifetime.

In happiness and peace.

Gautam Sachdeva
Mumbai, India
March 2001

FOREWORD

BY MARC ALLEN

Author of *Visionary Business* and *A Visionary Life*

Perhaps once in a decade, or even once in a generation, a book like *The Power of Now* comes along. It is more than a book; there is a living energy in it, one you can probably feel as you hold it. It has the power to create an experience in readers, and change their lives for the better.

The Power of Now was first published in Canada, and the Canadian publisher, Connie Kellough, told me she heard repeated stories of positive changes and even miracles that have happened once people got into the book. "Readers call in," she said. "And so many of them tell me of the wonderful healings, transformations, and increased joy they are experiencing because they have embraced this book."

The book makes me aware that every moment of my life is a miracle. This is absolutely true, whether I realize it or not. And *The Power of Now*, over and over, shows me how to realize it.

From the first page of his writing, it is clear that Eckhart Tolle is a contemporary master. He is not aligned with any particular religion or doctrine or guru; his teaching embraces the heart, the essence, of all other traditions, and contradicts none of them — Christian, Hindu, Buddhist, Muslim, indigenous, or anything else. He is able to do what all the great masters have done: to show us, in simple and clear language, that the way, the truth, and the light is within us.

Eckhart Tolle begins by briefly introducing us to his story — a story of early depression and despair that culminated in a tremendous experience of awakening one night not long after his twenty-ninth birthday. For the past twenty years, he has reflected on that experience, meditated, and deepened his understanding.

In the last decade, he has become a world-class teacher, a great soul with a great message, one that Christ taught, one that Buddha taught: a state of enlightenment is attainable, here and now. It is possible to live free of suffering, free of anxiety and neurosis. To do this, we have to come to understand our role as the creator of our pain; our own mind causes our problems, not other people, not "the world out there." It is our own mind, with its nearly constant stream of thoughts, thinking about the past, worrying about the future. We make the great mistake of identifying with our mind, thinking that's who we are — when, in fact, we are far greater beings.

Over and over, Eckhart Tolle shows us how to connect with what he calls our Being:

> Being is the eternal, ever-present One Life beyond the myriad forms of life that are subject to birth and death. However, Being is not only beyond but also deep within every form as its innermost invisible and indestructible essence. This means that it is accessible to you now as your own deepest self, your true nature. But don't seek to grasp it with your mind. Don't try to understand it. You can know it only when the mind is still, when you are present, fully and intensely in the Now....To regain awareness of Being and to abide in that state of 'feeling-realization' is enlightenment.

The Power of Now is nearly impossible to read straight through — it requires you to put it down periodically and reflect on the words and apply them to your own life experience. It is a complete guide, a complete course, in meditation and realization. It is a book to be revisited again and again — and each time you revisit it, you gain new depth and meaning. It is a book that many people, including me, will want to study for a lifetime.

The Power of Now has a growing number of devoted readers. It has already been called a masterpiece; whatever it is called, however it is described, it is a book with the power to change lives, the power to awaken us to fully realize who we are.

Marc Allen
Novato, California U.S.A.
August 1999

ACKNOWLEDGMENTS

I am deeply thankful to Connie Kellough for her loving support and her vital part in transforming the manuscript into this book and bringing it out into the world. It is a joy to work with her.

I extend my gratitude to Corea Ladner and those wonderful people who have contributed to this book by giving me *space*, that most precious of gifts — space to write and space to *be*. Thank you to Adrienne Bradley in Vancouver, to Margaret Miller in London and Angie Francesco in Glastonbury, England, Richard in Menlo Park and Rennie Frumkin in Sausalito, California.

I am also thankful to Shirley Spaxman and Howard Kellough for their early review of the manuscript and helpful feedback as well as to those individuals who were kind enough to review the manuscript at a later stage and provide additional input. Thank you to Rose Dendewich for word-processing the manuscript in her unique cheerful and professional manner.

Finally, I would like to express my love and gratitude to my mother and father, without whom this book would not have come into existence, to my spiritual teachers, and to the greatest guru of all: life.

THE POWER OF
NOW

INTRODUCTION

THE ORIGIN OF THIS BOOK

I have little use for the past and rarely think about it; however, I would briefly like to tell you how I came to be a spiritual teacher and how this book came into existence.

Until my thirtieth year, I lived in a state of almost continuous anxiety interspersed with periods of suicidal depression. It feels now as if I am talking about some past lifetime or somebody else's life.

One night not long after my twenty-ninth birthday, I woke up in the early hours with a feeling of absolute dread. I had woken up with such a feeling many times before, but this time it was more intense than it had ever been. The silence of the night, the vague outlines of the furniture in the dark room, the distant noise of a passing train — everything felt so alien, so hostile, and so utterly meaningless that it created in me a deep loathing of the world. The most loathsome thing of all, however, was my own existence. What was the point in continuing to live with this burden of misery? Why carry on with this continuous struggle? I could feel that a deep longing for annihilation, for nonexistence, was now becoming much stronger than the instinctive desire to continue to live.

"I cannot live with myself any longer." This was the thought that kept repeating itself in my mind. Then suddenly I became aware of what a peculiar thought it was. "Am I one or two? If I cannot live with myself, there must be two of me: the 'I' and the 'self' that 'I' cannot live with." "Maybe," I thought, "only one of them is real."

I was so stunned by this strange realization that my mind stopped. I was fully conscious, but there were no more thoughts. Then I felt drawn into what seemed like a vortex of energy. It was a slow movement at first and then accelerated. I was gripped by an intense fear, and my body started to shake. I heard the words "resist nothing," as if spoken inside my chest. I could feel myself being sucked into a void. It felt as if the void was inside myself rather than outside. Suddenly, there was no more fear, and I let myself fall into that void. I have no recollection of what happened after that.

I was awakened by the chirping of a bird outside the window. I had never heard such a sound before. My eyes were still closed, and I saw the image of a precious diamond. Yes, if a diamond could make a sound, this is what it would be like. I opened my eyes. The first light of dawn was filtering through the curtains. Without any thought, I felt, I knew, that there is infinitely more to light than we realize. That soft luminosity filtering through the curtains was love itself. Tears came into my eyes. I got up and walked around the room. I recognized the room, and yet I knew that I had never truly seen it before. Everything was fresh and pristine, as if it had just come into existence. I picked up things, a pencil, an empty bottle, marveling at the beauty and aliveness of it all.

That day I walked around the city in utter amazement at the miracle of life on earth, as if I had just been born into this world.

For the next five months, I lived in a state of uninterrupted deep peace and bliss. After that, it diminished somewhat in intensity, or perhaps it just seemed to because it became my natural state. I could still function in the world, although I realized that nothing I ever *did* could possibly add anything to what I already had.

I knew, of course, that something profoundly significant had happened to me, but I didn't understand it at all. It wasn't until several years later, after I had read spiritual texts and spent time with spiritual teachers, that I realized that what everybody was looking for had already happened to me. I understood that the intense pressure of suffering that night must have forced my consciousness to withdraw from its identification with the unhappy and deeply fearful self, which is ultimately a fiction of the mind. This withdrawal must have been so complete that this false, suffering self immediately collapsed, just as if a plug had been pulled out of an inflatable toy. What was left then was my true nature as the ever-present *I am:* consciousness in its pure state prior to identification with form. Later I also learned to go into that inner timeless and deathless realm that I had originally perceived as a void and remain fully conscious. I dwelt in states of such indescribable bliss and sacredness that even the original experience I just described pales in comparison. A time came when, for a while, I was left with nothing on the physical plane. I had no relationships, no job, no home, no socially defined identity. I spent almost two years sitting on park benches in a state of the most intense joy.

But even the most beautiful experiences come and go. More fundamental, perhaps, than any experience is the undercurrent of peace that has never left me since then. Sometimes it is very strong, almost palpable, and others can feel it too. At other times, it is somewhere in the background, like a distant melody.

Later, people would occasionally come up to me and say: "I want what you have. Can you give it to me, or show me how to get it?" And I would say: "You have it already. You just can't feel it because your mind is making too much noise." That answer later grew into the book that you are holding in your hands.

Before I knew it, I had an external identity again. I had become a spiritual teacher.

THE TRUTH THAT IS WITHIN YOU

This book represents the essence of my work, as far as it can be conveyed in words, with individuals and small groups of spiritual seekers during the past ten years, in Europe and in North America. In deep love and appreciation, I would like to thank those exceptional people for their courage, their willingness to embrace inner change, their challenging questions, and their readiness to listen. This book would not have come into existence without them. They belong to what is as yet a small but fortunately growing minority of spiritual pioneers: people who are reaching a point where they become capable of breaking out of inherited collective mind-patterns that have kept humans in bondage to suffering for eons.

I trust that this book will find its way to those who are ready for such radical inner transformation and so act as a catalyst for it. I also hope that it will reach many others who will find its content worthy of consideration, although they may not be ready to fully live or practice it. It is possible that at a later time, the seed that was sown when reading this book will merge with the seed of enlightenment that each human being carries within, and suddenly that seed will sprout and come alive within them.

The book in its present form originated, often spontaneously, in response to questions asked by individuals in seminars, meditation classes and private counseling sessions, and so I have kept the question-and-answer format. I learned and received as much in those classes and sessions as the questioners. Some of the questions and answers I wrote down almost verbatim. Others are generic, which is to say I combined certain types of questions that were frequently asked into one, and extracted the essence from different answers to form one generic answer. Sometimes, in the process of writing, an entirely new answer came that was more profound or insightful than anything I had ever uttered. Some additional questions were asked by the editor so as to provide further clarification of certain points.

You will find that from the first to the last page, the dialogues continuously alternate between two different levels.

On one level, I draw your attention to what is *false* in you. I speak of the nature of human unconsciousness and dysfunction as well as its most common behavioral manifestations, from conflict in relationships to warfare between tribes or nations. Such knowledge is vital, for unless you learn to recognize the false as false — as not you

— there can be no lasting transformation, and you would always end up being drawn back into illusion and into some form of pain. On this level, I also show you how not to make that which is false in you into a self and into a personal problem, for that is how the false perpetuates itself.

On another level, I speak of a profound transformation of human consciousness — not as a distant future possibility, but available now — no matter who or where you are. You are shown how to free yourself from enslavement to the mind, enter into this enlightened state of consciousness and sustain it in everyday life.

On this level of the book, the words are not always concerned with information, but often designed to draw you into this new consciousness as you read. Again and again, I endeavor to take you with me into that timeless state of intense conscious presence in the Now, so as to give you a taste of enlightenment. Until you are able to experience what I speak of, you may find those passages somewhat repetitive. As soon as you do, however, I believe you will realize that they contain a great deal of spiritual power, and they may become for you the most rewarding parts of the book. Moreover, since every person carries the seed of enlightenment within, I often address myself to the knower in you who dwells behind the thinker, the deeper self that immediately recognizes spiritual truth, resonates with it, and gains strength from it.

The pause symbol ∫ after certain passages is a suggestion that you may want to stop reading for a moment, become still, and feel and experience the truth of what has just been said. There may be other places in the text where you will do this naturally and spontaneously.

As you begin reading the book, the meaning of certain words, such as "Being" or "presence," may not be entirely clear to you at first. Just read on. Questions or objections may occasionally come into your mind as you read. They will probably be answered later in the book, or they may turn out to be irrelevant as you go more deeply into the teaching — and into yourself.

Don't read with the mind only. Watch out for any "feeling-response" as you read and a sense of recognition from deep within. I cannot tell you any spiritual truth that deep within you don't know already. All I can do is remind you of what you have forgotten. Living knowledge, ancient and yet ever new, is then activated and released from within every cell of your body.

The mind always wants to categorize and compare, but this book will work better for you if you do not attempt to compare its terminology with that of other teachings; otherwise, you will probably become confused. I use words such as "mind," "happiness," and "consciousness" in ways that do not necessarily correlate with other teachings. Don't get attached to any words. They are only stepping stones, to be left behind as quickly as possible.

When I occasionally quote the words of Jesus or the Buddha, from *A Course in Miracles* or from other teachings, I do so not in order to compare, but to draw your attention to the fact that in *essence* there is and always has been only one spiritual teaching, although it comes in many forms. Some of these forms, such as the ancient religions, have become so overlaid with extraneous matter that their spiritual essence has become almost completely obscured by it. To a large extent, therefore, their deeper meaning is no longer recognized and their transformative power lost. When I quote from the ancient religions or other teachings, it is to reveal their deeper meaning and thereby restore their transformative power — particularly for those readers who are followers of these religions or teachings. I say to them: there is no need to go elsewhere for the truth. Let me show you how to go more deeply into what you already have.

Mostly, however, I have endeavored to use terminology that is as neutral as possible in order to reach a wide range of people. This book can be seen as a restatement for our time of that one timeless spiritual teaching, the essence of all religions. It is not derived from external sources, but from the one true Source within, so it contains no theory or speculation. I speak from inner experience, and if at times I speak forcefully, it is to cut through heavy layers of mental resistance and to reach that place within you where you already *know*, just as I know, and where the truth is recognized when it is heard. There is then a feeling of exaltation and heightened aliveness, as something within you says: "Yes. I know this is true."

CHAPTER ONE

YOU ARE NOT YOUR MIND

THE GREATEST OBSTACLE TO ENLIGHTENMENT

Enlightenment — what is that?

A beggar had been sitting by the side of a road for over thirty years. One day a stranger walked by. "Spare some change?" mumbled the beggar, mechanically holding out his old baseball cap. "I have nothing to give you," said the stranger. Then he asked: "What's that you are sitting on?" "Nothing," replied the beggar. "Just an old box. I have been sitting on it for as long as I can remember." "Ever looked inside?" asked the stranger. "No," said the beggar. "What's the point? There's nothing in there." "Have a look inside," insisted the stranger. The beggar managed to pry open the lid. With astonishment, disbelief, and elation, he saw that the box was filled with gold.

I am that stranger who has nothing to give you and who is telling you to look inside. Not inside any box, as in the parable, but somewhere even closer: inside yourself.

"But I am not a beggar," I can hear you say.

Those who have not found their true wealth, which is the radiant joy of Being and the deep, unshakable peace that comes with it, are beggars, even if they have great material wealth. They are looking outside for scraps of pleasure or fulfillment, for validation, security, or love, while they have a treasure within that not only includes all those things but is infinitely greater than anything the world can offer.

THE POWER OF NOW

The word enlightenment conjures up the idea of some super-human accomplishment, and the ego likes to keep it that way, but it is simply your natural state of *felt* oneness with Being. It is a state of connectedness with something immeasurable and indestructible, something that, almost paradoxically, is essentially you and yet is much greater than you. It is finding your true nature beyond name and form. The inability to feel this connectedness gives rise to the illusion of separation, from yourself and from the world around you. You then perceive yourself, consciously or unconsciously, as an isolated fragment. Fear arises, and conflict within and without becomes the norm.

I love the Buddha's simple definition of enlightenment as "the end of suffering." There is nothing superhuman in that, is there? Of course, as a definition, it is incomplete. It only tells you what enlightenment is not: no suffering. But what's left when there is no more suffering? The Buddha is silent on that, and his silence implies that you'll have to find out for yourself. He uses a negative definition so that the mind cannot make it into something to believe in or into a superhuman accomplishment, a goal that is impossible for you to attain. Despite this precaution, the majority of Buddhists still believe that enlightenment is for the Buddha, not for them, at least not in this lifetime.

You used the word Being. *Can you explain what you mean by that?*

Being is the eternal, ever-present One Life beyond the myriad forms of life that are subject to birth and death. However, Being is not only beyond but also deep within every form as its innermost invisible and indestructible essence. This means that it is accessible to you now as your own deepest self, your true nature. But don't seek to grasp it with your mind. Don't try to understand it. You can know it only when the mind is still. When you are present, when your attention is fully and intensely in the Now, Being can be felt, but it can never be understood mentally. To regain awareness of Being and to abide in that state of "feeling-realization" is enlightenment.

10

$\int$

When you say Being, *are you talking about God? If you are, then why don't you say it?*

The word *God* has become empty of meaning through thousands of years of misuse. I use it sometimes, but I do so sparingly. By misuse, I mean that people who have never even glimpsed the realm of the sacred, the infinite vastness behind that word, use it with great conviction, as if they knew what they are talking about. Or they argue against it, as if they knew what it is that they are denying. This misuse gives rise to absurd beliefs, assertions, and egoic delusions, such as "*My* or *our* God is the only true God, and *your* God is false," or Nietzsche's famous statement "God is dead."

The word *God* has become a closed concept. The moment the word is uttered, a mental image is created, no longer, perhaps, of an old man with a white beard, but still a mental representation of someone or something outside you, and, yes, almost inevitably a *male* someone or something.

Neither *God* nor *Being* nor any other word can define or explain the ineffable reality behind the word, so the only important question is whether the word is a help or a hindrance in enabling you to experience That toward which it points. Does it point beyond itself to that transcendental reality, or does it lend itself too easily to becoming no more than an idea in your head that you believe in, a mental idol?

The word *Being* explains nothing, but nor does *God*. *Being*, however, has the advantage that it is an open concept. It does not reduce the infinite invisible to a finite entity. It is impossible to form a mental image of it. Nobody can claim exclusive possession of Being. It is your very essence, and it is immediately accessible to you as the feeling of your own presence, the realization *I am* that is prior to I am this or I am that. So it is only a small step from the word *Being* to the experience of Being.

11

∫

What is the greatest obstacle to experiencing this reality?

Identification with your mind, which causes thought to become compulsive. Not to be able to stop thinking is a dreadful affliction, but we don't realize this because almost everybody is suffering from it, so it is considered normal. This incessant mental noise prevents you from finding that realm of inner stillness that is inseparable from Being. It also creates a false mind-made self that casts a shadow of fear and suffering. We will look at all that in more detail later.

The philosopher Descartes believed that he had found the most fundamental truth when he made his famous statement: "I think, therefore I am." He had, in fact, given expression to the most basic error: to equate thinking with Being and identity with thinking. The compulsive thinker, which means almost everyone, lives in a state of apparent separateness, in an insanely complex world of continuous problems and conflict, a world that reflects the ever-increasing fragmentation of the mind. Enlightenment is a state of wholeness, of being "at one" and therefore at peace. At one with life in its manifested aspect, the world, as well as with your deepest self and life unmanifested — at one with Being. Enlightenment is not only the end of suffering and of continuous conflict within and without, but also the end of the dreadful enslavement to incessant thinking. What an incredible liberation this is!

Identification with your mind creates an opaque screen of concepts, labels, images, words, judgments, and definitions that blocks all true relationship. It comes between you and yourself, between you and your fellow man and woman, between you and nature, between you and God. It is this screen of thought that creates the illusion of separateness, the illusion that there is you *and* a totally separate "other." You then forget the essential fact that, underneath the level of physical appearances and separate forms, you are one with all that *is*. By "forget," I mean that you can no longer *feel* this oneness as self-evident reality. You may *believe* it to be true, but you no longer *know* it to be true. A belief may be comforting. Only through your own experience, however, does it become liberating.

Thinking has become a disease. Disease happens when things get out of balance. For example, there is nothing wrong with cells dividing and multiplying in the body, but when this process continues in disregard of the total organism, cells proliferate and we have disease.

Note: The mind is a superb instrument if used rightly. Used wrongly, however, it becomes very destructive. To put it more accurately, it is not so much that you use your mind wrongly — you usually don't use it at all. It uses *you*. This is the disease. You believe that you *are* your mind. This is the delusion. The instrument has taken you over.

I don't quite agree. It is true that I do a lot of aimless thinking, like most people, but I can still choose to use my mind to get and accomplish things, and I do that all the time.

Just because you can solve a crossword puzzle or build an atom bomb doesn't mean that you use your mind. Just as dogs love to chew bones, the mind loves to get its teeth into problems. That's why it does crossword puzzles and builds atom bombs. *You* have no interest in either. Let me ask you this: can you be free of your mind whenever you want to? Have you found the "off" button?

You mean stop thinking altogether? No, I can't, except maybe for a moment or two.

Then the mind is using you. You are unconsciously identified with it, so you don't even know that you are its slave. It's almost as if you were possessed without knowing it, and so you take the possessing entity to be yourself. The beginning of freedom is the realization that you are not the possessing entity — the thinker. Knowing this enables you to observe the entity. The moment you start *watching the thinker,* a higher level of consciousness becomes activated. You then begin to realize that there is a vast realm of intelligence beyond thought, that thought is only a tiny aspect of that intelligence. You also realize that all the things that truly matter — beauty, love, creativity, joy, inner peace — arise from beyond the mind. You begin to awaken.

$$\int$$

FREEING YOURSELF FROM YOUR MIND

What exactly do you mean by "watching the thinker"?

When someone goes to the doctor and says, "I hear a voice in my head," he or she will most likely be sent to a psychiatrist. The fact is that, in a very similar way, virtually everyone hears a voice, or several voices, in their head all the time: the involuntary thought processes that you don't realize you have the power to stop. Continuous monologues or dialogues.

You have probably come across "mad" people in the street incessantly talking or muttering to themselves. Well, that's not much different from what you and all other "normal" people do, except that you don't do it out loud. The voice comments, speculates, judges, compares, complains, likes, dislikes, and so on. The voice isn't necessarily relevant to the situation you find yourself in at the time; it may be reviving the recent or distant past or rehearsing or imagining possible future situations. Here it often imagines things going wrong and negative outcomes; this is called worry. Sometimes this soundtrack is accompanied by visual images or "mental movies."

14

Even if the voice is relevant to the situation at hand, it will interpret it in terms of the past. This is because the voice belongs to your conditioned mind, which is the result of all your past history as well as of the collective cultural mind-set you inherited. So you see and judge the present through the eyes of the past and get a totally distorted view of it. It is not uncommon for the voice to be a person's own worst enemy. Many people live with a tormentor in their head that continuously attacks and punishes them and drains them of vital energy. It is the cause of untold misery and unhappiness, as well as of disease.

The good news is that you *can* free yourself from your mind. This is the only true liberation. You can take the first step right now. Start listening to the voice in your head as often as you can. Pay particular attention to any repetitive thought patterns, those old gramophone records that have been playing in your head perhaps for many years. This is what I mean by "watching the thinker," which is another way of saying: listen to the voice in your head, *be* there as the witnessing presence.

When you listen to that voice, listen to it impartially. That is to say, do not judge. Do not judge or condemn what you hear, for doing so would mean that the same voice has come in again through the back door. You'll soon realize: *there* is the voice, and here *I am* listening to it, watching it. This *I am* realization, this sense of your own presence, is not a thought. It arises from beyond the mind.

So when you listen to a thought, you are aware not only of the thought but also of yourself as the witness of the thought. A new dimension of consciousness has come in. As you listen to the thought, you feel a conscious presence — your deeper self — behind or underneath the thought, as it were. The thought then loses its power over you and quickly subsides, because you are no longer energizing the mind through identification with it. This is the beginning of the end of involuntary and compulsive thinking.

When a thought subsides, you experience a discontinuity in the mental stream — a gap of "no-mind." At first, the gaps will be short, a few seconds perhaps, but gradually they will become longer. When these gaps occur, you feel a certain stillness and peace inside you. This is the beginning of your natural state of felt oneness with Being, which is usually obscured by the mind. With practice, the sense of stillness and peace will deepen. In fact, there is no end to its depth. You will also feel a subtle emanation of joy arising from deep within: the joy of Being.

It is not a trancelike state. Not at all. There is no loss of consciousness here. The opposite is the case. If the price of peace were a lowering of your consciousness, and the price of stillness a lack of vitality and alertness, then they would not be worth having. In this state of inner connectedness, you are much more alert, more awake than in the mind-identified state. You are fully present. It also raises the vibrational frequency of the energy field that gives life to the physical body.

As you go more deeply into this realm of no-mind, as it is sometimes called in the East, you realize the state of pure consciousness. In that state, you feel your own presence with such intensity and such joy that all thinking, all emotions, your physical body, as well as the whole external world become relatively insignificant in comparison to it. And yet this is not a selfish but a selfless state. It takes you beyond what you previously thought of as "your self." That presence is essentially you and at the same time inconceivably greater than you. What I am trying to convey here may sound paradoxical or even contradictory, but there is no other way that I can express it.

Instead of "watching the thinker," you can also create a gap in the mind stream simply by directing the focus of your attention into the Now. Just become intensely conscious of the present moment. This is a deeply satisfying thing to do. In this way, you draw consciousness away from mind activity and create a gap of no-mind in which you are highly alert and aware but not thinking. This is the essence of meditation.

In your everyday life, you can practice this by taking any routine activity that normally is only a means to an end and giving it your fullest attention, so that it becomes an end in itself. For example, every time you walk up and down the stairs in your house or place of work, pay close attention to every step, every movement, even your breathing. Be totally present. Or when you wash your hands, pay attention to all the sense perceptions associated with the activity: the sound and feel of the water, the movement of your hands, the scent of the soap, and so on. Or when you get into your car, after you close the door, pause for a few seconds and observe the flow of your breath. Become aware of a silent but powerful sense of presence. There is one certain criterion by which you can measure your success in this practice: the degree of peace that you feel within.

So the single most vital step on your journey toward enlightenment is this: learn to disidentify from your mind. Every time you create a gap in the stream of mind, the light of your consciousness grows stronger.

One day you may catch yourself smiling at the voice in your head, as you would smile at the antics of a child. This means that you no longer take the content of your mind all that seriously, as your sense of self does not depend on it.

ENLIGHTENMENT: RISING ABOVE THOUGHT

Isn't thinking essential in order to survive in this world?

Your mind is an instrument, a tool. It is there to be used for a specific task, and when the task is completed, you lay it down. As it is, I would say about 80 to 90 percent of most people's thinking is not only repetitive and useless, but because of its dysfunctional and often negative nature, much of it is also harmful. Observe your mind and you will find this to be true. It causes a serious leakage of vital energy.

This kind of compulsive thinking is actually an addiction. What characterizes an addiction? Quite simply this: you no longer feel that you have the choice to stop. It seems stronger than you. It also gives you a false sense of pleasure, pleasure that invariably turns into pain.

Why should we be addicted to thinking?

Because you are identified with it, which means that you derive your sense of self from the content and activity of your mind. Because you believe that you would cease to be if you stopped thinking. As you grow up, you form a mental image of who you are, based on your personal and cultural conditioning. We may call this phantom self the ego. It consists of mind activity and can only be kept going through constant thinking. The term ego means different things to different people, but when I use it here it means a false self, created by unconscious identification with the mind.

To the ego, the present moment hardly exists. Only past and future are considered important. This total reversal of the truth accounts for the fact that in the ego mode the mind is so dysfunctional. It is always concerned with keeping the past alive, because without it — who are you? It constantly projects itself into the future to ensure its continued survival and to seek some kind of release or fulfillment there. It says: "One day, when this, that, or the other happens, I am going to be okay, happy, at peace." Even when the ego seems to be concerned with the present, it is not the present that it

sees: It misperceives it completely because it looks at it t
eyes of the past. Or it reduces the present to a means to an e
that always lies in the mind-projected future. Observe your
you'll see that this is how it works.

The present moment holds the key to liberation. But you cannot
find the present moment as long as you *are* your mind.

I don't want to lose my ability to analyze and discriminate. I would-
n't mind learning to think more clearly, in a more focused way, but I
don't want to lose my mind. The gift of thought is the most precious
thing we have. Without it, we would just be another species of animal.

The predominance of mind is no more than a stage in the evolution
of consciousness. We need to go on to the next stage now as a matter
of urgency; otherwise, we will be destroyed by the mind, which has
grown into a monster. I will talk about this in more detail later.
Thinking and consciousness are not synonymous. Thinking is only a
small aspect of consciousness. Thought cannot exist without consciousness, but consciousness does not need thought.

Enlightenment means rising above thought, not falling back to a
level below thought, the level of an animal or a plant. In the enlightened state, you still use your thinking mind when needed, but in a
much more focused and effective way than before. You use it mostly
for practical purposes, but you are free of the involuntary internal dia-
logue, and there is inner stillness. When you do use your mind, and
particularly when a creative solution is needed, you oscillate every few
minutes or so between thought and stillness, between mind and no-
mind. No-mind is consciousness without thought. Only in that way
is it possible to think creatively, because only in that way does
thought have any real power. Thought alone, when it is no longer
connected with the much vaster realm of consciousness, quickly
becomes barren, insane, destructive.

The mind is essentially a survival machine. Attack and defense
against other minds, gathering, storing, and analyzing information
— this is what it is good at, but it is not at all creative. All true artists,

whether they know it or not, create from a place of no-mind, from inner stillness. The mind then gives form to the creative impulse or insight. Even the great scientists have reported that their creative breakthroughs came at a time of mental quietude. The surprising result of a nation-wide inquiry among America's most eminent mathematicians, including Einstein, to find out their working methods, was that thinking "plays only a subordinate part in the brief, decisive phase of the creative act itself."[1] So I would say that the simple reason why the majority of scientists are *not* creative is not because they don't know how to think but because they don't know how to stop thinking!

It wasn't through the mind, through thinking, that the miracle that is life on earth or your body were created and are being sustained. There is clearly an intelligence at work that is far greater than the mind. How can a single human cell measuring $1/1,000$ of an inch across contain instructions within its DNA that would fill $1,000$ books of 600 pages each? The more we learn about the workings of the body, the more we realize just how vast is the intelligence at work within it and how little we know. When the mind reconnects with that, it becomes a most wonderful tool. It then serves something greater than itself.

EMOTION: THE BODY'S REACTION TO YOUR MIND

What about emotions? I get caught up in my emotions more than I do in my mind.

Mind, in the way I use the word, is not just thought. It includes your emotions as well as all unconscious mental-emotional reactive patterns. Emotion arises at the place where mind and body meet. It is the body's reaction to your mind — or you might say, a reflection of your mind in the body. For example, an attack thought or a hostile thought will create a build-up of energy in the body that we call anger. The body is getting ready to fight. The thought that you are being threatened, physically or psychologically, causes the body to contract, and this is the physical side of what we call fear. Research has shown that strong emotions even cause changes in the biochemistry of the body. These biochemical changes represent the physical or material aspect of the emotion. Of course, you are not usually conscious of all your thought patterns, and it is often only through watching your emotions that you can bring them into awareness.

The more you are identified with your thinking, your likes and dislikes, judgments and interpretations, which is to say the less *present* you are as the watching consciousness, the stronger the emotional energy charge will be, whether you are aware of it or not. If you cannot feel your emotions, if you are cut off from them, you will eventually experience them on a purely physical level, as a physical problem or symptom. A great deal has been written about this in recent years, so we don't need to go into it here. A strong unconscious emotional pattern may even manifest as an external event that appears to just happen to you. For example, I have observed that people who carry a lot of anger inside without being aware of it and without expressing it are more likely to be attacked, verbally or even physically, by other angry people, and often for no apparent reason. They have a strong emanation of anger that certain people pick up subliminally and that triggers their own latent anger.

If you have difficulty feeling your emotions, start by focusing attention on the inner energy field of your body. Feel the body from within. This will also put you in touch with your emotions. We will explore this in more detail later.

You say that an emotion is the mind's reflection in the body. But sometimes there is a conflict between the two: the mind says "no" while the emotion says "yes," or the other way around.

If you really want to know your mind, the body will always give you a truthful reflection, so look at the emotion or rather *feel* it in your body. If there is an apparent conflict between them, the thought will be the lie, the emotion will be the truth. Not the ultimate truth of who you are, but the relative truth of your state of mind at that time.

Conflict between surface thoughts and unconscious mental processes is certainly common. You may not yet be able to bring your unconscious mind activity into awareness *as thoughts*, but it will always be reflected in the body *as an emotion*, and of this you *can* become aware. To watch an emotion in this way is basically the same as listening to or watching a thought, which I described earlier. The only difference is that, while a thought is in your head, an emotion has a strong physical component and so is primarily felt in the body. You can then allow the emotion to *be* there without being controlled by it. You no longer *are* the emotion; you are the watcher, the observing presence. If you practice this, all that is unconscious in you will be brought into the light of consciousness.

So observing our emotions is as important as observing our thoughts?

Yes. Make it a habit to ask yourself: What's going on inside me at this moment? That question will point you in the right direction. But don't analyze, just watch. Focus your attention within. Feel the energy of the emotion. If there is no emotion present, take your attention more deeply into the inner energy field of your body. It is the doorway into Being.

An emotion usually represents an amplified and energized thought pattern, and because of its often overpowering energetic charge, it is not easy initially to stay present enough to be able to watch it. It wants to take you over, and it usually succeeds — unless there is enough presence in you. If you are pulled into unconscious identification

22

with the emotion through lack of presence, which is normal, the emotion temporarily becomes "you." Often a vicious circle builds up between your thinking and the emotion: they feed each other. The thought pattern creates a magnified reflection of itself in the form of an emotion, and the vibrational frequency of the emotion keeps feeding the original thought pattern. By dwelling mentally on the situation, event, or person that is the perceived cause of the emotion, the thought feeds energy to the emotion, which in turn energizes the thought pattern, and so on.

Basically, all emotions are modifications of one primordial, undifferentiated emotion that has its origin in the loss of awareness of who you are beyond name and form. Because of its undifferentiated nature, it is hard to find a name that precisely describes this emotion. "Fear" comes close, but apart from a continuous sense of threat, it also includes a deep sense of abandonment and incompleteness. It may be best to use a term that is as undifferentiated as that basic emotion and simply call it "pain." One of the main tasks of the mind is to fight or remove that emotional pain, which is one of the reasons for its incessant activity, but all it can ever achieve is to cover it up temporarily. In fact, the harder the mind struggles to get rid of the pain, the greater the pain. The mind can never find the solution, nor can it afford to allow you to find the solution, because it is itself an intrinsic part of the "problem." Imagine a chief of police trying to find an arsonist when the arsonist *is* the chief of police. You will not be free of that pain until you cease to derive your sense of self from identification with the mind, which is to say from ego. The mind is then toppled from its place of power and Being reveals itself as your true nature.

Yes, I know what you are going to ask.

I was going to ask: What about positive emotions such as love and joy?

They are inseparable from your natural state of inner connectedness with Being. Glimpses of love and joy or brief moments of deep peace are possible whenever a gap occurs in the stream of thought. For most people, such gaps happen rarely and only accidentally, in moments when the mind is rendered "speechless," sometimes triggered by great beauty, extreme physical exertion, or even great danger. Suddenly, there is inner stillness. And within that stillness there is a subtle but intense joy, there is love, there is peace.

Usually, such moments are short-lived, as the mind quickly resumes its noise-making activity that we call thinking. Love, joy, and peace cannot flourish until you have freed yourself from mind dominance. But they are not what I would call emotions. They lie beyond the emotions, on a much deeper level. So you need to become fully conscious of your emotions and be able to *feel* them before you can feel that which lies beyond them. Emotion literally means "disturbance." The word comes from the Latin *emovere*, meaning "to disturb."

Love, joy, and peace are deep states of Being or rather three aspects of the state of inner connectedness with Being. As such, they have no opposite. This is because they arise from beyond the mind. Emotions, on the other hand, being part of the dualistic mind, are subject to the law of opposites. This simply means that you cannot have good without bad. So in the unenlightened, mind-identified condition, what is sometimes wrongly called joy is the usually short-lived pleasure side of the continuously alternating pain/pleasure cycle. Pleasure is always derived from something outside you, whereas joy arises from within. The very thing that gives you pleasure today will give you pain tomorrow, or it will leave you, so its absence will give you pain. And what is often referred to as love may be pleasurable and exciting for a while, but it is an addictive clinging, an extremely needy condition that can turn into its opposite at the flick of a switch. Many "love" relationships, after the initial euphoria has passed, actually oscillate between "love" and hate, attraction and attack.

Real love doesn't make you suffer. How could it? It doesn't suddenly turn into hate, nor does real joy turn into pain. As I said, even before you are enlightened — before you have freed yourself from your mind — you may get glimpses of true joy, true love, or of a deep inner peace, still but vibrantly alive. These are aspects of your true nature, which is usually obscured by the mind. Even within a "normal" addictive relationship, there can be moments when the presence of something more genuine, something incorruptible, can be felt. But they will only be glimpses, soon to be covered up again through mind interference. It may then seem that you had something very precious and lost it, or your mind may convince you that it was all an illusion anyway. The truth is that it wasn't an illusion, and you cannot lose it. It is part of your natural state, which can be obscured but can never be destroyed by the mind. Even when the sky is heavily overcast, the sun hasn't disappeared. It's still there on the other side of the clouds.

The Buddha says that pain or suffering arises through desire or craving and that to be free of pain we need to cut the bonds of desire.

All cravings are the mind seeking salvation or fulfillment in external things and in the future as a substitute for the joy of Being. As long as I am my mind, I am those cravings, those needs, wants, attachments, and aversions, and apart from them there is no "I" except as a mere possibility, an unfulfilled potential, a seed that has not yet sprouted. In that state, even my desire to become free or enlightened is just another craving for fulfillment or completion in the future. So don't seek to become free of desire or "achieve" enlightenment. Become present. Be there as the observer of the mind. Instead of quoting the Buddha, *be* the Buddha, *be* "the awakened one," which is what the word *buddha* means.

Humans have been in the grip of pain for eons, ever since they fell from the state of grace, entered the realm of time and mind, and lost awareness of Being. At that point, they started to perceive themselves as meaningless fragments in an alien universe, unconnected to the Source and to each other.

Pain is inevitable as long as you are identified with your mind, which is to say as long as you are unconscious, spiritually speaking.

I am talking here primarily of emotional pain, which is also the main cause of physical pain and physical disease. Resentment, hatred, self-pity, guilt, anger, depression, jealousy, and so on, even the slightest irritation, are all forms of pain. And every pleasure or emotional high contains within itself the seed of pain: its inseparable opposite, which will manifest in time.

Anybody who has ever taken drugs to get "high" will know that the high eventually turns into a low, that the pleasure turns into some form of pain. Many people also know from their own experience how easily and quickly an intimate relationship can turn from a source of pleasure to a source of pain. Seen from a higher perspective, both the negative and the positive polarities are faces of the same coin, are both part of the underlying pain that is inseparable from the mind-identified egoic state of consciousness.

There are two levels to your pain: the pain that you create now, and the pain from the past that still lives on in your mind and body. Ceasing to create pain in the present and dissolving past pain — this is what I want to talk about now.

CHAPTER TWO

CONSCIOUSNESS: THE WAY OUT OF PAIN

CREATE NO MORE PAIN IN THE PRESENT

Nobody's life is entirely free of pain and sorrow. Isn't it a question of learning to live with them rather than trying to avoid them?

The greater part of human pain is unnecessary. It is self-created as long as the unobserved mind runs your life.

The pain that you create now is always some form of nonacceptance, some form of unconscious resistance to what *is*. On the level of thought, the resistance is some form of judgment. On the emotional level, it is some form of negativity. The intensity of the pain depends on the degree of resistance to the present moment, and this in turn depends on how strongly you are identified with your mind. The mind always seeks to deny the Now and to escape from it. In other words, the more you are identified with your mind, the more you suffer. Or you may put it like this: the more you are able to honor and accept the Now, the more you are free of pain, of suffering — and free of the egoic mind.

Why does the mind habitually deny or resist the Now? Because it cannot function and remain in control without time, which is past and future, so it perceives the timeless Now as threatening. Time and mind are in fact inseparable.

Imagine the Earth devoid of human life, inhabited only by plants and animals. Would it still have a past and a future? Could we still speak of time in any meaningful way? The question "What time is it?" or "What's the date today?" — if anybody were there to ask it — would be quite meaningless. The oak tree or the eagle would be bemused by such a question. "What time?" they would ask. "Well, of course, it's now. The time is now. What else is there?"

Yes, we need the mind as well as time to function in this world, but there comes a point where they take over our lives, and this is where dysfunction, pain, and sorrow set in.

The mind, to ensure that it remains in control, seeks continuously to cover up the present moment with past and future, and so, as the vitality and infinite creative potential of Being, which is inseparable from the Now, becomes covered up by time, your true nature becomes obscured by the mind. An increasingly heavy burden of time has been accumulating in the human mind. All individuals are suffering under this burden, but they also keep adding to it every moment whenever they ignore or deny that precious moment or reduce it to a means of getting to some future moment, which only exists in the mind, never in actuality. The accumulation of time in the collective and individual human mind also holds a vast amount of residual pain from the past.

If you no longer want to create pain for yourself and others, if you no longer want to add to the residue of past pain that still lives on in you, then don't create any more time, or at least no more than is necessary to deal with the practical aspects of your life. How to stop creating time? Realize deeply that the present moment is all you ever have. Make the Now the primary focus of your life. Whereas before you dwelt in time and paid brief visits to the Now, have your dwelling place in the Now and pay brief visits to past and future when required to deal with the practical aspects of your life situation. Always say "yes" to the present moment. What could be more futile, more insane, than to create inner resistance to something that already *is*? What could be more insane than to oppose life itself, which is now and always now? Surrender to what *is*. Say "yes" to life — and see how life suddenly starts working *for* you rather than against you.

∫

The present moment is sometimes unacceptable, unpleasant, or awful.

It is as it is. Observe how the mind labels it and how this labeling process, this continuous sitting in judgment, creates pain and unhappiness. By watching the mechanics of the mind, you step out of its resistance patterns, and you can then *allow the present moment to be*. This will give you a taste of the state of inner freedom from external conditions, the state of true inner peace. Then see what happens, and take action if necessary or possible.

Accept — then act. Whatever the present moment contains, accept it as if you had chosen it. Always work with it, not against it. Make it your friend and ally, not your enemy. This will miraculously transform your whole life.

∫

PAST PAIN: DISSOLVING THE PAIN-BODY

As long as you are unable to access the power of the Now, every emotional pain that you experience leaves behind a residue of pain that lives on in you. It merges with the pain from the past, which was already there, and becomes lodged in your mind and body. This, of course, includes the pain you suffered as a child, caused by the unconsciousness of the world into which you were born.

This accumulated pain is a negative energy field that occupies your body and mind. If you look on it as an invisible entity in its own right, you are getting quite close to the truth. It's the emotional pain-

29

body. It has two modes of being: dormant and active. A pain-body may be dormant 90 percent of the time; in a deeply unhappy person, though, it may be active up to 100 percent of the time. Some people live almost entirely through their pain-body, while others may experience it only in certain situations, such as intimate relationships, or situations linked with past loss or abandonment, physical or emotional hurt, and so on. Anything can trigger it, particularly if it resonates with a pain pattern from your past. When it is ready to awaken from its dormant stage, even a thought or an innocent remark made by someone close to you can activate it.

Some pain-bodies are obnoxious but relatively harmless, for example like a child who won't stop whining. Others are vicious and destructive monsters, true demons. Some are physically violent; many more are emotionally violent. Some will attack people around you or close to you, while others may attack you, their host. Thoughts and feelings you have about your life then become deeply negative and self-destructive. Illnesses and accidents are often created in this way. Some pain-bodies drive their hosts to suicide.

When you thought you knew a person and then you are suddenly confronted with this alien, nasty creature for the first time, you are in for quite a shock. However, it's more important to observe it in yourself than in someone else. Watch out for any sign of unhappiness in yourself, in whatever form — it may be the awakening pain-body. This can take the form of irritation, impatience, a somber mood, a desire to hurt, anger, rage, depression, a need to have some drama in your relationship, and so on. Catch it the moment it awakens from its dormant state.

The pain-body wants to survive, just like every other entity in existence, and it can only survive if it gets you to unconsciously identify with it. It can then rise up, take you over, "become you," and live through you. It needs to get its "food" through you. It will feed on any experience that resonates with its own kind of energy, anything that creates further pain in whatever form: anger, destructiveness, hatred, grief, emotional drama, violence, and even illness. So the pain-body, when it has taken you over, will create a situation in your life that reflects back its own energy frequency for it to feed on. Pain can only feed on pain. Pain cannot feed on joy. It finds it quite indigestible.

Once the pain-body has taken you over, you want more pain. You become a victim or a perpetrator. You want to inflict pain, or you want to suffer pain, or both. There isn't really much difference between the two. You are not conscious of this, of course, and will vehemently claim that you do not want pain. But look closely and you will find that your thinking and behavior are designed to keep the pain going, for yourself and others. If you *were* truly conscious of it, the pattern would dissolve, for to want more pain is insanity, and nobody is consciously insane.

The pain-body, which is the dark shadow cast by the ego, is actually afraid of the light of your consciousness. It is afraid of being found out. Its survival depends on your unconscious identification with it, as well as on your unconscious fear of facing the pain that lives in you. But if you don't face it, if you don't bring the light of your consciousness into the pain, you will be forced to relive it again and again. The pain-body may seem to you like a dangerous monster that you cannot bear to look at, but I assure you that it is an insubstantial phantom that cannot prevail against the power of your presence.

Some spiritual teachings state that all pain is ultimately an illusion, and this is true. The question is: Is it true for you? A mere belief doesn't make it true. Do you want to experience pain for the rest of your life and keep saying that it is an illusion? Does that free you from the pain? What we are concerned with here is how you can *realize* this truth — that is, make it real in your own experience.

So the pain-body doesn't want you to observe it directly and see it for what it is. The moment you observe it, feel its energy field within you, and take your attention into it, the identification is broken. A higher dimension of consciousness has come in. I call it *presence*. You are now the witness or the watcher of the pain-body. This means that it cannot use you anymore by pretending to be you, and it can no longer replenish itself through you. You have found your own innermost strength. You have accessed the power of Now.

What happens to the pain-body when we become conscious enough to break our identification with it?

Unconsciousness creates it; consciousness transmutes it into itself. St. Paul expressed this universal principle beautifully: "Everything is shown up by being exposed to the light, and whatever is exposed to the light itself becomes light." Just as you cannot fight the darkness, you cannot fight the pain-body. Trying to do so would create inner conflict and thus further pain. Watching it is enough. Watching it implies accepting it as part of what *is* at that moment.

The pain-body consists of trapped life-energy that has split off from your total energy field and has temporarily become autonomous through the unnatural process of mind identification. It has turned in on itself and become anti-life, like an animal trying to devour its own tail. Why do you think our civilization has become so life-destructive? But even the life-destructive forces are still life-energy.

When you start to disidentify and become the watcher, the pain-body will continue to operate for a while and will try to trick you into identifying with it again. Although you are no longer energizing it through your identification, it has a certain momentum, just like a spinning wheel that will keep turning for a while even when it is no longer being propelled. At this stage, it may also create physical aches and pains in different parts of the body, but they won't last. Stay present, stay conscious. Be the ever-alert guardian of your inner space. You need to be present enough to be able to watch the pain-body directly and feel its energy. It then cannot control your thinking. The moment your thinking is aligned with the energy field of the pain-body, you are identified with it and again feeding it with your thoughts.

For example, if anger is the predominant energy vibration of the pain-body and you think angry thoughts, dwelling on what someone did to you or what you are going to do to him or her, then you have become unconscious, and the pain-body has become "you." Where there is anger, there is always pain underneath. Or when a dark mood comes upon you and you start getting into a negative mind-pattern and thinking how dreadful your life is, your thinking has become aligned with the pain-body, and you have become unconscious and vulnerable to the pain-body's attack. "Unconscious," the way that I use the word here, means to be identified with some mental or emotional pattern. It implies a complete absence of the watcher.

Sustained conscious attention severs the link between the pain-body and your thought processes and brings about the process of transmutation. It is as if the pain becomes fuel for the flame of your consciousness, which then burns more brightly as a result. This is the esoteric meaning of the ancient art of alchemy: the transmutation of base metal into gold, of suffering into consciousness. The split within is healed, and you become whole again. Your responsibility then is not to create further pain.

Let me summarize the process. Focus attention on the feeling inside you. Know that it is the pain-body. Accept that it is there. Don't *think* about it — don't let the feeling turn into thinking. Don't judge or analyze. Don't make an identity for yourself out of it. Stay present, and continue to be the observer of what is happening inside you. Become aware not only of the emotional pain but also of "the one who observes," the silent watcher. This is the power of the Now, the power of your own conscious presence. Then see what happens.

For many women, the pain-body awakens particularly at the time preceding the menstrual flow. I will talk about this and the reason for it in more detail later. Right now, let me just say this: If you are able to stay alert and present at that time and *watch* whatever you feel within, rather than be taken over by it, it affords an opportunity for the most powerful spiritual practice, and a rapid transmutation of all past pain becomes possible.

EGO IDENTIFICATION WITH THE PAIN-BODY

The process that I have just described is profoundly powerful yet simple. It could be taught to a child, and hopefully one day it will be one of the first things children learn in school. Once you have understood the basic principle of being present as the watcher of what happens inside you — and you "understand" it by experiencing it — you have at your disposal the most potent transformational tool.

This is not to deny that you may encounter intense inner resistance to disidentifying from your pain. This will be the case particularly if you have lived closely identified with your emotional pain-body for most of your life and the whole or a large part of your sense of self is invested in it. What this means is that you have made an unhappy self out of your pain-body and believe that this mind-made fiction is who you are. In that case, unconscious fear of losing your identity will create strong resistance to any disidentification. In other words, you would rather be in pain — *be* the pain-body — than take a leap into the unknown and risk losing the familiar unhappy self.

If this applies to you, observe the resistance within yourself. Observe the attachment to your pain. Be very alert. Observe the peculiar pleasure you derive from being unhappy. Observe the compulsion to talk or think about it. The resistance will cease if you make it conscious. You can then take your attention into the pain-body, stay present as the witness, and so initiate its transmutation.

Only *you* can do this. Nobody can do it *for* you. But if you are fortunate enough to find someone who is intensely conscious, if you can be with them and join them in the state of presence, that can be helpful and will accelerate things. In this way, your own light will quickly grow stronger. When a log that has only just started to burn is placed next to one that is burning fiercely, and after a while they are separated again, the first log will be burning with much greater intensity. After all, it is the same fire. To be such a fire is one of the functions of a spiritual teacher. Some therapists may also be able to fulfill that function, provided that they have gone beyond the level of mind and can create and sustain a state of intense conscious presence while they are working with you.

THE ORIGIN OF FEAR

You mentioned fear as being part of our basic underlying emotional pain. How does fear arise, and why is there so much of it in people's lives? And isn't a certain amount of fear just healthy self-protection? If I didn't have a fear of fire, I might put my hand in it and get burned.

The reason why you don't put your hand in the fire is not because of fear, it's because you know that you'll get burned. You don't need fear to avoid unnecessary danger — just a minimum of intelligence and common sense. For such practical matters, it is useful to apply the lessons learned in the past. Now if someone *threatened* you with fire or with physical violence, you might experience something like fear. This is an instinctive shrinking back from danger, but not the psychological condition of fear that we are talking about here. The psychological condition of fear is divorced from any concrete and true immediate danger. It comes in many forms: unease, worry, anxiety, nervousness, tension, dread, phobia, and so on. This kind of psychological fear is always of something that *might* happen, not of something that is happening now. *You* are in the here and now, while your mind is in the future. This creates an anxiety gap. And if you are identified with your mind and have lost touch with the power and simplicity of the Now, that anxiety gap will be your constant companion. You can always cope with the present moment, but you cannot cope with something that is only a mind projection — you cannot cope with the future.

Moreover, as long as you are identified with your mind, the ego runs your life, as I pointed out earlier. Because of its phantom nature, and despite elaborate defense mechanisms, the ego is very vulnerable and insecure, and it sees itself as constantly under threat. This, by the way, is the case even if the ego is outwardly very confident. Now remember that an emotion is the body's reaction to your mind. What message is the body receiving continuously from the ego, the false, mind-made self? Danger, I am under threat. And what is the emotion generated by this continuous message? Fear, of course.

Fear seems to have many causes. Fear of loss, fear of failure, fear of being hurt, and so on, but ultimately all fear is the ego's fear of death, of annihilation. To the ego, death is always just around the corner. In this mind-identified state, fear of death affects every aspect of your life. For example, even such a seemingly trivial and "normal" thing as the compulsive need to be right in an argument and make the other person wrong — defending the mental position with which you have identified — is due to the fear of death. If you identify with a mental position, then if you are wrong, your mind-based sense of self is seriously threatened with annihilation. So you as the ego cannot afford to be wrong. To be wrong is to die. Wars have been fought over this, and countless relationships have broken down.

Once you have disidentified from your mind, whether you are right or wrong makes no difference to your sense of self at all, so the forcefully compulsive and deeply unconscious need to be right, which is a form of violence, will no longer be there. You can state clearly and firmly how you feel or what you think, but there will be no aggressiveness or defensiveness about it. Your sense of self is then derived from a deeper and truer place within yourself, not from the mind. Watch out for any kind of defensiveness within yourself. What are you defending? An illusory identity, an image in your mind, a fictitious entity. By making this pattern conscious, by witnessing it, you disidentify from it. In the light of your consciousness, the unconscious pattern will then quickly dissolve. This is the end of all arguments and power games, which are so corrosive to relationships. Power over others is weakness disguised as strength. True power is within, and it is available to you now.

So anyone who is identified with their mind and, therefore, disconnected from their true power, their deeper self rooted in Being, will have fear as their constant companion. The number of people who have gone beyond mind is as yet extremely small, so you can assume that virtually everyone you meet or know lives in a state of fear. Only the intensity of it varies. It fluctuates between anxiety and dread at one end of the scale and a vague unease and distant sense of threat at the other. Most people become conscious of it only when it takes on one of its more acute forms.

THE EGO'S SEARCH FOR WHOLENESS

Another aspect of the emotional pain that is an intrinsic part of the egoic mind is a deep-seated sense of lack or incompleteness, of not being whole. In some people, this is conscious, in others unconscious. If it is conscious, it manifests as the unsettling and constant feeling of not being worthy or good enough. If it is unconscious, it will only be felt indirectly as an intense craving, wanting and needing. In either case, people will often enter into a compulsive pursuit of ego-gratification and things to identify with in order to fill this hole they feel within. So they strive after possessions, money, success, power, recognition, or a special relationship, basically so that they can feel better about themselves, feel more complete. But even when they attain all these things, they soon find that the hole is still there, that it is bottomless. Then they are really in trouble, because they cannot delude themselves anymore. Well, they can and do, but it gets more difficult.

As long as the egoic mind is running your life, you cannot truly be at ease; you cannot be at peace or fulfilled except for brief intervals when you obtained what you wanted, when a craving has just been fulfilled. Since the ego is a derived sense of self, it needs to identify with external things. It needs to be both defended and fed constantly. The most common ego identifications have to do with possessions, the work you do, social status and recognition, knowledge and education, physical appearance, special abilities, relationships, personal and family history, belief systems, and often also political, nationalistic, racial, religious, and other collective identifications. None of these is you.

Do you find this frightening? Or is it a relief to know this? All of these things you will have to relinquish sooner or later. Perhaps you find it as yet hard to believe, and I am certainly not asking you to *believe* that your identity cannot be found in any of those things. You will *know* the truth of it for yourself. You will know it at the latest when you feel death approaching. Death is a stripping away of all that is not you. The secret of life is to "die before you die" — and find that there is no death.

CHAPTER THREE

MOVING DEEPLY INTO THE NOW

DON'T SEEK YOUR SELF IN THE MIND

I feel that there is still a great deal I need to learn about the workings of my mind before I can get anywhere near full consciousness or spiritual enlightenment.

No, you don't. The problems of the mind cannot be solved on the level of the mind. Once you have understood the basic dysfunction, there isn't really much else that you need to learn or understand. Studying the complexities of the mind may make you a good psychologist, but doing so won't take you beyond the mind, just as the study of madness isn't enough to create sanity. You have already understood the basic mechanics of the unconscious state: identification with the mind, which creates a false self, the ego, as a substitute for your true self rooted in Being. You become as a "branch cut off from the vine," as Jesus puts it.

The ego's needs are endless. It feels vulnerable and threatened and so lives in a state of fear and want. Once you know how the basic dysfunction operates, there is no need to explore all its countless manifestations, no need to make it into a complex personal problem. The ego, of course, loves that. It is always seeking for something to attach itself to in order to uphold and strengthen its illusory sense of self, and it will readily attach itself to your problems. This is why, for so many people, a large part of their sense of self is intimately connected with their problems. Once this has happened, the last thing they want is to become free of them; that would mean loss of self. There can be a great deal of unconscious ego investment in pain and suffering.

So once you recognize the root of unconsciousness as identification with the mind, which of course includes the emotions, you step out of it. You become *present*. When you are present, you can allow the mind to be as it is without getting entangled in it. The mind in itself is not dysfunctional. It is a wonderful tool. Dysfunction sets in when you seek your self in it and mistake it for who you are. It then becomes the *egoic* mind and takes over your whole life.

END THE DELUSION OF TIME

It seems almost impossible to disidentify from the mind. We are all immersed in it. How do you teach a fish to fly?

Here is the key: End the delusion of time. Time and mind are inseparable. Remove time from the mind and it stops — unless you choose to use it.

To be identified with your mind is to be trapped in time: the compulsion to live almost exclusively through memory and anticipation. This creates an endless preoccupation with past and future and an unwillingness to honor and acknowledge the present moment and *allow it to be*. The compulsion arises because the past gives you an identity and the future holds the promise of salvation, of fulfillment in whatever form. Both are illusions.

But without a sense of time, how would we function in this world? There would be no goals to strive toward anymore. I wouldn't even know who I am, because my past makes me who I am today. I think time is something very precious, and we need to learn to use it wisely rather than waste it.

Time isn't precious at all, because it is an illusion. What you perceive as precious is not time but the one point that is out of time: the Now. That is precious indeed. The more you are focused on time — past and future — the more you miss the Now, the most precious thing there is.

Why is it the most precious thing? Firstly, because it is the *only* thing. It's all there is. The eternal present is the space within which your whole life unfolds, the one factor that remains constant. Life is now. There was never a time when your life was *not* now, nor will there ever be. Secondly, the Now is the only point that can take you beyond the limited confines of the mind. It is your only point of access into the timeless and formless realm of Being.

$$\int$$

NOTHING EXISTS OUTSIDE THE NOW

Aren't past and future just as real, sometimes even more real, than the present? After all, the past determines who we are, as well as how we perceive and behave in the present. And our future goals determine which actions we take in the present.

You haven't yet grasped the essence of what I am saying because you are trying to understand it mentally. The mind cannot understand this. Only *you* can. Please just listen.

Have you ever experienced, done, thought, or felt anything outside the Now? Do you think you ever will? Is it possible for anything to happen or *be* outside the Now? The answer is obvious, is it not?

Nothing ever happened in the past; it happened in the Now.

Nothing will ever happen in the future; it will happen in the Now.

What you think of as the past is a memory trace, stored in the mind, of a former Now. When you remember the past, you reactivate a memory trace — and you do so now. The future is an imagined Now, a projection of the mind. When the future comes, it comes as the Now. When you think about the future, you do it now. Past and future obviously have no reality of their own. Just as the moon has no light of its own, but can only reflect the light of the sun, so are past and future only pale reflections of the light, power, and reality of the eternal present. Their reality is "borrowed" from the Now.

The essence of what I am saying here cannot be understood by the mind. The moment you grasp it, there is a shift in consciousness from mind to Being, from time to presence. Suddenly, everything feels alive, radiates energy, emanates Being.

THE KEY TO THE SPIRITUAL DIMENSION

In life-threatening emergency situations, the shift in consciousness from time to presence sometimes happens naturally. The personality that has a past and a future momentarily recedes and is replaced by an intense conscious presence, very still but very alert at the same time. Whatever response is needed then arises out of that state of consciousness.

The reason why some people love to engage in dangerous activities, such as mountain climbing, car racing, and so on, although they may not be aware of it, is that it forces them into the Now — that intensely alive state that is free of time, free of problems, free of thinking, free of the burden of the personality. Slipping away from the present moment even for a second may mean death. Unfortunately, they come to depend on a particular activity to be in that state. But you don't need to climb the north face of the Eiger. You can enter that state now.

Since ancient times, spiritual masters of all traditions have pointed to the Now as the key to the spiritual dimension. Despite this, it seems to have remained a secret. It is certainly not taught in churches and temples. If you go to a church, you may hear readings from the Gospels such as "Take no thought for the morrow; for the morrow shall take thought for the things of itself," or "Nobody who puts his hands to the plow and *looks back* is fit for the Kingdom of God." Or you might hear the passage about the beautiful flowers that are not anxious about tomorrow but live with ease in the timeless Now and are provided for abundantly by God. The depth and radical nature of these teachings are not recognized. No one seems to realize that they are meant to be lived and so bring about a profound inner transformation.

The whole essence of Zen consists in walking along the razor's edge of Now — to be so utterly, so completely *present* that no problem, no suffering, nothing that is not *who you are* in your essence, can survive in you. In the Now, in the absence of time, all your problems dissolve. Suffering needs time; it cannot survive in the Now.

The great Zen master Rinzai, in order to take his students' attention away from time, would often raise his finger and slowly ask: "What, at this moment, is lacking?" A powerful question that does not require an answer on the level of the mind. It is designed to take your attention deeply into the Now. A similar question in the Zen tradition is this: "If not now, when?"

The Now is also central to the teaching of Sufism, the mystical branch of Islam. Sufis have a saying: "The Sufi is the son of time present." And Rumi, the great poet and teacher of Sufism, declares: "Past and future veil God from our sight; burn up both of them with fire."

Meister Eckhart, the thirteenth-century spiritual teacher, summed it all up beautifully: "Time is what keeps the light from reaching us. There is no greater obstacle to God than time."

∫

ACCESSING THE POWER OF THE NOW

A moment ago, when you talked about the eternal present and the unreality of past and future, I found myself looking at that tree outside the window. I had looked at it a few times before, but this time it was different. The external perception had not changed much, except that the colors seemed brighter and more vibrant. But there was now an added dimension to it. This is hard to explain. I don't know how, but I was aware of something invisible that I felt was the essence of that tree, its inner spirit, if you like. And somehow I was part of that. I realize now that I hadn't truly seen the tree before, just a flat and dead image of it. When I look at the tree now, some of that awareness is still present, but I can feel it slipping away. You see, the experience is already receding into the past. Can something like this ever be more than a fleeting glimpse?

You were free of time for a moment. You moved into the Now and therefore perceived the tree without the screen of mind. The awareness of Being became part of your perception. With the timeless dimension comes a different kind of knowing, one that does not "kill" the spirit that lives within every creature and every thing. A knowing that does not destroy the sacredness and mystery of life but contains a deep love and reverence for all that *is*. A knowing of which the mind knows nothing.

The mind cannot know the tree. It can only know facts or information *about* the tree. My mind cannot know *you*, only labels, judgments, facts, and opinions *about* you. Being alone knows directly.

There is a place for mind and mind knowledge. It is in the practical realm of day-to-day living. However, when it takes over all aspects of your life, including your relationships with other human beings and with nature, it becomes a monstrous parasite that, unchecked, may well end up killing all life on the planet and finally itself by killing its host.

You have had a glimpse of how the timeless can transform your perceptions. But an experience is not enough, no matter how beautiful or profound. What is needed and what we are concerned with is a permanent shift in consciousness.

So break the old pattern of present-moment denial and present-moment resistance. Make it your practice to withdraw attention from past and future whenever they are not needed. Step out of the time dimension as much as possible in everyday life. If you find it hard to enter the Now directly, start by observing the habitual tendency of your mind to want to escape from the Now. You will observe that the future is usually imagined as either better or worse than the present. If the imagined future is better, it gives you hope or pleasurable anticipation. If it is worse, it creates anxiety. Both are illusory. Through self-observation, more *presence* comes into your life automatically. The moment you realize you are not present, you *are* present. Whenever you are able to observe your mind, you are no longer trapped in it. Another factor has come in, something that is not of the mind: the witnessing presence.

Be present as the watcher of your mind — of your thoughts and emotions as well as your reactions in various situations. Be at least as interested in your reactions as in the situation or person that causes you to react. Notice also how often your attention is in the past or future. Don't judge or analyze what you observe. Watch the thought,

45

feel the emotion, observe the reaction. Don't make a personal problem out of them. You will then feel something more powerful than any of those things that you observe: the still, observing presence itself behind the content of your mind, the silent watcher.

∫

Intense presence is needed when certain situations trigger a reaction with a strong emotional charge, such as when your self-image is threatened, a challenge comes into your life that triggers fear, things "go wrong," or an emotional complex from the past is brought up. In those instances, the tendency is for you to become "unconscious." The reaction or emotion takes you over — you "become" it. You act it out. You justify, make wrong, attack, defend...except that it isn't you, it's the reactive pattern, the mind in its habitual survival mode.

Identification with the mind gives it more energy; observation of the mind withdraws energy from it. Identification with the mind creates more time; observation of the mind opens up the dimension of the timeless. The energy that is withdrawn from the mind turns into presence. Once you can feel what it means to be present, it becomes much easier to simply choose to step out of the time dimension whenever time is not needed for practical purposes and move more deeply into the Now. This does not impair your ability to use time — past or future — when you need to refer to it for practical matters. Nor does it impair your ability to use your mind. In fact, it enhances it. When you do use your mind, it will be sharper, more focused.

LETTING GO OF PSYCHOLOGICAL TIME

Learn to use time in the practical aspects of your life — we may call this "clock time" — but immediately return to present-moment awareness when those practical matters have been dealt with. In this

way, there will be no build-up of "psychological time," which is identification with the past and continuous compulsive projection into
the future.

Clock time is not just making an appointment or planning a trip.
It includes learning from the past so that we don't repeat the same
mistakes over and over. Setting goals and working toward them.
Predicting the future by means of patterns and laws, physical, math-
ematical and so on, learned from the past and taking appropriate
action on the basis of our predictions.

But even here, within the sphere of practical living, where we
cannot do without reference to past and future, the present moment
remains the essential factor: Any lesson from the past becomes relevant and is applied *now*. Any planning as well as working toward
achieving a particular goal is done *now*.

The enlightened person's main focus of attention is always the
Now, but they are still peripherally aware of time. In other words,
they continue to use clock time but are free of psychological time.

Be alert as you practice this so that you do not unwittingly transform clock time into psychological time. For example, if you made a
mistake in the past and learn from it now, you are using clock time.
On the other hand, if you dwell on it mentally, and self-criticism,
remorse, or guilt come up, then you are making the mistake into
"me" and "mine": you make it part of your sense of self, and it has
become psychological time, which is always linked to a false sense of
identity. Nonforgiveness necessarily implies a heavy burden of psychological time.

If you set yourself a goal and work toward it, you are using clock
time. You are aware of where you want to go, but you honor and give
your fullest attention to the step that you are taking at this moment.
If you then become excessively focused on the goal, perhaps because
you are seeking happiness, fulfillment, or a more complete sense of
self in it, the Now is no longer honored. It becomes reduced to a mere
stepping stone to the future, with no intrinsic value. Clock time then
turns into psychological time. Your life's journey is no longer an

adventure, just an obsessive need to arrive, to attain, to "make it." You no longer see or smell the flowers by the wayside either, nor are you aware of the beauty and the miracle of life that unfolds all around you when you are present in the Now.

∫

I can see the supreme importance of the Now, but I cannot quite go along with you when you say that time is a complete illusion.

When I say "time is an illusion," my intention is not to make a philosophical statement. I am just reminding you of a simple fact — a fact so obvious that you may find it hard to grasp and may even find it meaningless — but once fully realized, it can cut like a sword through all the mind-created layers of complexity and "problems." Let me say it again: the present moment is all you ever have. There is never a time when your life is not "this moment." Is this not a fact?

THE INSANITY OF PSYCHOLOGICAL TIME

You will not have any doubt that psychological time is a mental disease if you look at its collective manifestations. They occur, for example, in the form of ideologies such as communism, national socialism or any nationalism, or rigid religious belief systems, which operate under the implicit assumption that the highest good lies in the future and that therefore the end justifies the means. The end is an idea, a point in the mind-projected future, when salvation in whatever form — happiness, fulfillment, equality, liberation, and so on — will be attained. Not infrequently, the means of getting there are the enslavement, torture, and murder of people in the present.

For example, it is estimated that as many as 50 million people were murdered to further the cause of communism, to bring about a "better world" in Russia, China, and other countries.[2] This is a chilling example of how belief in a future heaven creates a present hell. Can there be any doubt that psychological time is a serious and dangerous mental illness?

How does this mind pattern operate in *your* life? Are you always trying to get somewhere other than where you are? Is most of your *doing* just a means to an end? Is fulfillment always just around the corner or confined to short-lived pleasures, such as sex, food, drink, drugs, or thrills and excitement? Are you always focused on becoming, achieving, and attaining, or alternatively chasing some new thrill or pleasure? Do you believe that if you acquire more things you will become more fulfilled, good enough, or psychologically complete? Are you waiting for a man or woman to give meaning to your life?

In the normal, mind-identified or unenlightened state of consciousness, the power and infinite creative potential that lie concealed in the Now are completely obscured by psychological time. Your life then loses its vibrancy, its freshness, its sense of wonder. The old patterns of thought, emotion, behavior, reaction, and desire are acted out in endless repeat performances, a script in your mind that gives you an identity of sorts but distorts or covers up the reality of the Now. The mind then creates an obsession with the future as an escape from the unsatisfactory present.

NEGATIVITY AND SUFFERING HAVE THEIR ROOTS IN TIME

But the belief that the future will be better than the present is not always an illusion. The present can be dreadful, and things can get better in the future, and often they do.

Usually, the future is a replica of the past. Superficial changes are possible, but *real* transformation is rare and depends upon whether you can become present enough to dissolve the past by accessing the power of the Now. What you perceive as future is an intrinsic part of your state of consciousness now. If your mind carries a heavy burden of past, you will experience more of the same. The past perpetuates itself through lack of presence. The quality of your consciousness at this moment is what shapes the future — which, of course, can only be experienced as the Now.

You may win $10 million, but that kind of change is no more than skin deep. You would simply continue to act out the same conditioned patterns in more luxurious surroundings. Humans have learned to split the atom. Instead of killing ten or twenty people with a wooden club, one person can now kill a million just by pushing a button. Is that *real* change?

If it is the quality of your consciousness at this moment that determines the future, then what is it that determines the quality of your consciousness? Your degree of presence. So the only place where true change can occur and where the past can be dissolved is the Now.

$$\int$$

All negativity is caused by an accumulation of psychological time and denial of the present. Unease, anxiety, tension, stress, worry — all forms of fear — are caused by too much future, and not enough presence. Guilt, regret, resentment, grievances, sadness, bitterness, and all forms of nonforgiveness are caused by too much past, and not enough presence.

Most people find it difficult to believe that a state of consciousness totally free of all negativity is possible. And yet this is the liberated state to which all spiritual teachings point. It is the promise of salvation, not in an illusory future but right here and now.

You may find it hard to recognize that time is the cause of your suffering or your problems. You believe that they are caused by specific situations in your life, and seen from a conventional viewpoint, this is true. But until you have dealt with the basic problem-making dysfunction of the mind — its attachment to past and future and denial of the Now — problems are actually interchangeable. If all your problems or perceived causes of suffering or unhappiness were miraculously removed for you today, but you had not become more present, more conscious, you would soon find yourself with a similar set of problems or causes of suffering, like a shadow that follows you wherever you go. Ultimately, there is only one problem: the time-bound mind itself.

I cannot believe that I could ever reach a point where I am completely free of my problems.

You are right. You can never *reach* that point because you *are* at that point *now*.

There is no salvation in time. You cannot be free in the future. Presence is the key to freedom, so you can only be free now.

FINDING THE LIFE UNDERNEATH YOUR LIFE SITUATION

I don't see how I can be free now. As it happens, I am extremely unhappy with my life at the moment. This is a fact, and I would be deluding myself if I tried to convince myself that all is well when it definitely isn't. To me, the present moment is very unhappy; it is not liberating at all. What keeps me going is the hope or possibility of some improvement in the future.

You think that your attention is in the present moment when it's actually taken up completely by time. You cannot be both unhappy *and* fully present in the Now.

What you refer to as your "life" should more accurately be called your "life situation." It is psychological time: past and future. Certain things in the past didn't go the way you wanted them to go. You are still resisting what happened in the past, and now you are resisting what *is*. Hope is what keeps you going, but hope keeps you focused on the future, and this continued focus perpetuates your denial of the Now and therefore your unhappiness.

It is true that my present life situation is the result of things that happened in the past, but it is still my present situation, and being stuck in it is what makes me unhappy.

Forget about your life situation for a while and pay attention to your *life*.

What is the difference?

Your life situation exists in time.
Your life is now.
Your life situation is mind-stuff.
Your life is real.
Find the "narrow gate that leads to life." It is called the Now. Narrow your life down to this moment. Your life situation may be full of problems — most life situations are — but find out if you have any problem at this moment. Not tomorrow or in ten minutes, but now. Do you have a problem now?
When you are full of problems, there is no room for anything new to enter, no room for a solution. So whenever you can, make some room, create some space, so that you find the life underneath your life situation.
Use your senses fully. Be where you are. Look around. Just look, don't interpret. See the light, shapes, colors, textures. Be aware of the silent presence of each thing. Be aware of the space that allows everything to be. Listen to the sounds; don't judge them. Listen to the silence underneath the sounds. Touch something — anything — and feel and acknowledge its Being. Observe the rhythm of your breathing; feel the air flowing in and out, feel the life energy inside your body. Allow everything to be, within and without. Allow the "isness" of all things. Move deeply into the Now.
You are leaving behind the deadening world of mental abstraction,

of time. You are getting out of the insane mind that is draining you of life energy, just as it is slowly poisoning and destroying the Earth. You are awakening out of the dream of time into the present.

ALL PROBLEMS ARE ILLUSIONS OF THE MIND

It feels as if a heavy burden has been lifted. A sense of lightness. I feel clear... but my problems are still there waiting for me, aren't they? They haven't been solved. Am I not just temporarily evading them?

If you found yourself in paradise, it wouldn't be long before your mind would say "yes, but...." Ultimately, this is not about solving your problems. It's about realizing that there *are* no problems. Only situations — to be dealt with now, or to be left alone and accepted as part of the "isness" of the present moment until they change or *can* be dealt with. Problems are mind-made and need time to survive. They cannot survive in the actuality of the Now.

Focus your attention on the Now and tell me what problem you have at this moment.

I am not getting any answer because it is impossible to have a problem when your attention is fully in the Now. A situation that needs to be either dealt with or accepted — yes. Why make it into a problem? Why make anything into a problem? Isn't life challenging enough as it is? What do you need problems for? The mind unconsciously loves problems because they give you an identity of sorts. This is normal, and it is insane. "Problem" means that you are dwelling on a situation mentally without there being a true intention or possibility of taking action now and that you are unconsciously making it part of your sense of self. You become so overwhelmed by your life situation that you lose your sense of life, of Being. Or you are carrying in your mind the insane burden of a hundred things that you will or may have to do in the future instead of focusing your attention on the one thing that you *can* do now.

When you create a problem, you create pain. All it takes is a simple choice, a simple decision: no matter what happens, I will create no more pain for myself. I will create no more problems. Although it is a simple choice, it is also very radical. You won't make that choice unless you are truly fed up with suffering, unless you have truly had enough. And you won't be able to go through with it unless you access the power of the Now. If you create no more pain for yourself, then you create no more pain for others. You also no longer contaminate the beautiful Earth, your inner space, and the collective human psyche with the negativity of problem-making.

If you have ever been in a life-or-death emergency situation, you will know that it wasn't a problem. The mind didn't have *time* to fool around and make it into a problem. In a true emergency, the mind stops; you become totally present in the Now, and something infinitely more powerful takes over. This is why there are many reports of ordinary people suddenly becoming capable of incredibly courageous deeds. In any emergency, either you survive or you don't. Either way, it is not a problem.

Some people get angry when they hear me say that problems are illusions. I am threatening to take away their sense of who they are. They have invested much time in a false sense of self. For many years, they have unconsciously defined their whole identity in terms of their problems or their suffering. Who would they be without it?

A great deal of what people say, think, or do is actually motivated by fear, which of course is always linked with having your focus on the future and being out of touch with the Now. As there are no problems in the Now, there is no fear either.

Should a situation arise that you need to deal with now, your action will be clear and incisive if it arises out of present-moment awareness. It is also more likely to be effective. It will not be a reaction coming from the past conditioning of your mind but an intuitive response to the situation. In other instances, when the time-bound mind would have reacted, you will find it more effective to do nothing — just stay centered in the Now.

A QUANTUM LEAP IN THE EVOLUTION OF CONSCIOUSNESS

I have had glimpses of this state of freedom from mind and time that you describe, but past and future are so overwhelmingly strong that I cannot keep them out for long.

The time-bound mode of consciousness is deeply embedded in the human psyche. But what we are doing here is part of a profound transformation that is taking place in the collective consciousness of the planet and beyond: the awakening of consciousness from the dream of matter, form, and separation. The ending of time. We are breaking mind patterns that have dominated human life for eons. Mind patterns that have created unimaginable suffering on a vast scale. I am not using the word evil. It is more helpful to call it unconsciousness or insanity.

This breaking up of the old mode of consciousness or rather unconsciousness: is it something we have to do or will it happen anyway? I mean, is this change inevitable?

That's a question of perspective. The doing and the happening is in fact a single process; because you are one with the totality of consciousness, you cannot separate the two. But there is no absolute guarantee that humans will make it. The process isn't inevitable or automatic. Your cooperation is an essential part of it. However you look at it, it is a quantum leap in the evolution of consciousness, as well as our only chance of survival as a race.

THE JOY OF BEING

To alert you that you have allowed yourself to be taken over by psychological time, you can use a simple criterion. Ask yourself: Is there joy, ease, and lightness in what I am doing? If there isn't, then time is covering up the present moment, and life is perceived as a burden or a struggle.

If there is no joy, ease, or lightness in what you are doing, it does not necessarily mean that you need to change *what* you are doing. It may be sufficient to change the *how*. "How" is always more important than "what." See if you can give much more attention to the *doing* than to the result that you want to achieve through it. Give your fullest attention to whatever the moment presents. This implies that you also completely accept what *is*, because you cannot give your full attention to something and at the same time resist it.

As soon as you honor the present moment, all unhappiness and struggle dissolve, and life begins to flow with joy and ease. When you act out of present-moment awareness, whatever you do becomes imbued with a sense of quality, care, and love — even the most simple action.

So do not be concerned with the fruit of your action — just give attention to the action itself. The fruit will come of its own accord. This is a powerful spiritual practice. In the *Bhagavad Gita*, one of the oldest and most beautiful spiritual teachings in existence, non-attachment to the fruit of your action is called Karma Yoga. It is described as the path of "consecrated action."

When the compulsive striving away from the Now ceases, the joy of Being flows into everything you do. The moment your attention turns to the Now, you feel a presence, a stillness, a peace. You no longer depend on the future for fulfillment and satisfaction — you don't look to it for salvation. Therefore, you are not attached to the results. Neither failure nor success has the power to change your inner state of Being. You have found the life underneath your life situation.

In the absence of psychological time, your sense of self is derived from Being, not from your personal past. Therefore, the psychological need to become anything other than who you are already is no longer there. In the world, on the level of your life situation, you may indeed become wealthy, knowledgeable, successful, free of this or that, but in the deeper dimension of Being you are complete and whole *now*.

In that state of wholeness, would we still be able or willing to pursue external goals?

Of course, but you will not have illusory expectations that anything or anybody in the future will save you or make you happy. As far as your life situation is concerned, there may be things to be attained or acquired. That's the world of form, of gain and loss. Yet on a deeper level you are already complete, and when you realize that, there is a playful, joyous energy behind what you do. Being free of psychological time, you no longer pursue your goals with grim determination, driven by fear, anger, discontent, or the need to become someone. Nor will you remain inactive through fear of failure, which to the ego is loss of self. When your deeper sense of self is derived from Being, when you are free of "becoming" as a psychological need, neither your happiness nor your sense of self depends on the outcome, and so there is freedom from fear. You don't seek permanency where it cannot be found: in the world of form, of gain and loss, birth and death. You don't demand that situations, conditions, places, or people should make you happy, and then suffer when they don't live up to your expectations.

Everything is honored, but nothing matters. Forms are born and die, yet you are aware of the eternal underneath the forms. You know that "nothing real can be threatened." [3]

When this is your state of Being, how can you not succeed? You have succeeded already.

CHAPTER FOUR

MIND STRATEGIES FOR
AVOIDING THE NOW

LOSS OF NOW: THE CORE DELUSION

Even if I completely accept that ultimately time is an illusion, what difference is that going to make in my life? I still have to live in a world that is completely dominated by time.

Intellectual agreement is just another belief and won't make much difference to your life. To realize this truth, you need to live it. When every cell of your body is so present that it feels vibrant with life, and when you can feel that life every moment as the joy of Being, then it can be said that you are free of time.

But I still have to pay the bills tomorrow, and I am still going to grow old and die just like everybody else. So how can I ever say that I am free of time?

Tomorrow's bills are not the problem. The dissolution of the physical body is not a problem. Loss of Now is the problem, or rather: the core delusion that turns a mere situation, event, or emotion into a personal problem and into suffering. Loss of Now is loss of Being.

To be free of time is to be free of the psychological need of past for your identity and future for your fulfillment. It represents the most profound transformation of consciousness that you can imagine. In some rare cases, this shift in consciousness happens dramatically and radically, once and for all. When it does, it usually comes about through total surrender in the midst of intense suffering. Most people, however, have to work at it.

When you have had your first few glimpses of the timeless state of consciousness, you begin to move back and forth between the dimensions of time and presence. First you become aware of just how rarely your attention is truly in the Now. But to *know* that you are *not* present is a great success: that knowing *is* presence — even if initially it only lasts for a couple of seconds of clock time before it is lost again. Then, with increasing frequency, you *choose* to have the focus of your consciousness in the present moment rather than in the past or future, and whenever you realize that you had lost the Now, you are able to stay in it not just for a couple of seconds, but for longer periods as perceived from the external perspective of clock time. So before you are firmly established in the state of presence, which is to say before you are fully conscious, you shift back and forth for a while between consciousness and unconsciousness, between the state of presence and the state of mind identification. You lose the Now, and you return to it, again and again. Eventually, presence becomes your predominant state.

For most people, presence is experienced either never at all or only accidentally and briefly on rare occasions without being recognized for what it is. Most humans alternate not between consciousness and unconsciousness but only between different levels of unconsciousness.

ORDINARY UNCONSCIOUSNESS AND DEEP UNCONSCIOUSNESS

What do you mean by different levels of unconsciousness?

As you probably know, in sleep you constantly move between the phases of dreamless sleep and the dream state. Similarly, in wakefulness most people only shift between ordinary unconsciousness and deep unconsciousness. What I call ordinary unconsciousness means being identified with your thought processes and emotions, your reactions, desires, and aversions. It is most people's normal state. In that state, you are run by the egoic mind, and you are unaware of Being. It is a state not of acute pain or unhappiness but of an almost continuous low level of unease, discontent, boredom, or nervousness — a kind of background static. You may not realize this because it is so much a part of "normal" living, just as you are not aware of a continuous low background noise, such as the hum of an air conditioner, until it stops. When it suddenly does stop, there is a sense of relief. Many people use alcohol, drugs, sex, food, work, television, or even shopping as anesthetics in an unconscious attempt to remove the basic unease. When this happens, an activity that might be very enjoyable if used in moderation becomes imbued with a compulsive or addictive quality, and all that is ever achieved through it is extremely short-lived symptom relief.

The unease of ordinary unconsciousness turns into the pain of deep unconsciousness — a state of more acute and more obvious suffering or unhappiness — when things "go wrong," when the ego is threatened or there is a major challenge, threat, or loss, real or imagined, in your life situation or conflict in a relationship. It is an intensified version of ordinary unconsciousness, different from it not in kind but in degree.

In ordinary unconsciousness, habitual resistance to or denial of what *is* creates the unease and discontent that most people accept as normal living. When this resistance becomes intensified through some challenge or threat to the ego, it brings up intense negativity such as anger, acute fear, aggression, depression, and so on. Deep unconsciousness often means that the pain-body has been triggered and that you have become identified with it. Physical violence would be impossible without deep unconsciousness. It can also occur easily whenever and wherever a crowd of people or even an entire nation generates a negative collective energy field.

The best indicator of your level of consciousness is how you deal with life's challenges when they come. Through those challenges, an already unconscious person tends to become more deeply unconscious, and a conscious person more intensely conscious. You can use a challenge to awaken you, or you can allow it to pull you into even deeper sleep. The dream of ordinary unconsciousness then turns into a nightmare.

If you cannot be present even in normal circumstances, such as when you are sitting alone in a room, walking in the woods, or listening to someone, then you certainly won't be able to stay conscious when something "goes wrong" or you are faced with difficult people or situations, with loss or the threat of loss. You will be taken over by a reaction, which ultimately is always some form of fear, and pulled into deep unconsciousness. Those challenges are your tests. Only the way in which you deal with them will show you and others where you are at as far as your state of consciousness is concerned, not how long you can sit with your eyes closed or what visions you see.

So it is essential to bring more consciousness into your life in ordinary situations when everything is going relatively smoothly. In this way, you grow in presence power. It generates an energy field in you and around you of a high vibrational frequency. No unconsciousness, no negativity, no discord or violence can enter that field and survive, just as darkness cannot survive in the presence of light.

When you learn to be the witness of your thoughts and emotions, which is an essential part of being present, you may be surprised when you first become aware of the background "static" of ordinary unconsciousness and realize how rarely, if ever, you are truly at ease within yourself. On the level of your thinking, you will find a great deal of resistance in the form of judgment, discontent, and mental projection away from the Now. On the emotional level, there will be an undercurrent of unease, tension, boredom, or nervousness. Both are aspects of the mind in its habitual resistance mode.

WHAT ARE THEY SEEKING?

Carl Jung tells in one of his books of a conversation he had with a Native American chief who pointed out to him that in his perception most white people have tense faces, staring eyes, and a cruel demeanor. He said: "They are always seeking something. What are they seeking? The whites always want something. They are always uneasy and restless. We don't know what they want. We think they are mad."

The undercurrent of constant unease started long before the rise of Western industrial civilization, of course, but in Western civilization, which now covers almost the entire globe, including most of the East, it manifests in an unprecedentedly acute form. It was already there at the time of Jesus, and it was there 600 years before that at the time of Buddha, and long before that. Why are you always anxious? Jesus asked his disciples. "Can anxious thought add a single day to your life?" And the Buddha taught that the root of suffering is to be found in our constant wanting and craving.

Resistance to the Now as a collective dysfunction is intrinsically connected to loss of awareness of Being and forms the basis of our dehumanized industrial civilization. Freud, by the way, also recognized the existence of this undercurrent of unease and wrote about it in his book *Civilization and Its Discontents*, but he did not recognize the true root of the unease and failed to realize that freedom from it is possible. This collective dysfunction has created a very unhappy and extraordinarily violent civilization that has become a threat not only to itself but also to all life on the planet.

DISSOLVING ORDINARY UNCONSCIOUSNESS

So how can we be free of this affliction?

Make it conscious. Observe the many ways in which unease, discontent, and tension arise within you through unnecessary judgment, resistance to what *is*, and denial of the Now. Anything unconscious dissolves when you shine the light of consciousness on it. Once you know how to dissolve ordinary unconsciousness, the light of your presence will shine brightly, and it will be much easier to deal with deep unconsciousness whenever you feel its gravitational pull.

However, ordinary unconsciousness may not be easy to detect initially because it is so normal.

Make it a habit to monitor your mental-emotional state through self-observation. "Am I at ease at this moment?" is a good question to ask yourself frequently. Or you can ask: "What's going on inside me at this moment?" Be at least as interested in what goes on inside you as what happens outside. If you get the inside right, the outside will fall into place. Primary reality is within, secondary reality without. But don't answer these questions immediately. Direct your attention inward. Have a look inside yourself. What kind of thoughts is your mind producing? What do you feel? Direct your attention into the body. Is there any tension? Once you detect that there is a low level of unease, the background static, see in what way you are avoiding, resisting, or denying life — by denying the Now. There are many ways in which people unconsciously resist the present moment. I will give you a few examples. With practice, your power of self-observation, of monitoring your inner state, will become sharpened.

FREEDOM FROM UNHAPPINESS

Do you resent doing what you are doing? It may be your job, or you may have agreed to do something and are doing it, but part of you resents and resists it. Are you carrying unspoken resentment toward a person close to you? Do you realize that the energy you thus emanate is so harmful in its effects that you are in fact contaminating yourself as well as those around you? Have a good look inside. Is there even the slightest trace of resentment, unwillingness? If there is, observe it on both the mental and the emotional levels. What thoughts is your mind creating around this situation? Then look at the emotion, which is the body's reaction to those thoughts. Feel the emotion. Does it feel pleasant or unpleasant? Is it an energy that you would actually *choose* to have inside you? Do you *have* a choice?

Maybe you *are* being taken advantage of, maybe the activity you are engaged in *is* tedious, maybe someone close to you *is* dishonest, irritating, or unconscious, but all this is irrelevant. Whether your thoughts and emotions about this situation are justified or not makes no difference. The fact is that you are resisting what *is*. You are making the present moment into an enemy. You are creating unhappiness, conflict between the inner and the outer. Your unhappiness is polluting not only your own inner being and those around you but also the collective human psyche of which you are an inseparable part. The pollution of the planet is only an outward reflection of an inner psychic pollution: millions of unconscious individuals not taking responsibility for their inner space.

Either stop doing what you are doing, speak to the person concerned and express fully what you feel, or drop the negativity that your mind has created around the situation and that serves no purpose whatsoever except to strengthen a false sense of self. Recognizing its futility is important. Negativity is never the optimum way of dealing with any situation. In fact, in most cases it keeps you stuck in it, blocking real change. Anything that is done with negative energy will become contaminated by it and in time give rise to more pain, more unhappiness. Furthermore, any negative inner state is contagious: Unhappiness spreads more easily than a physical disease. Through the law of resonance, it triggers and feeds latent negativity in others, unless they are immune — that is, highly conscious.

Are you polluting the world or cleaning up the mess? You are responsible for your inner space; nobody else is, just as you are responsible for the planet. As within, so without: If humans clear inner pollution, then they will also cease to create outer pollution.

How can we drop negativity, as you suggest?

By dropping it. How do you drop a piece of hot coal that you are holding in your hand? How do you drop some heavy and useless baggage that you are carrying? By recognizing that you don't want to suffer the pain or carry the burden anymore and then letting go of it.

Deep unconsciousness, such as the pain-body, or other deep pain, such as the loss of a loved one, usually needs to be transmuted through acceptance combined with the light of your presence — your sustained attention. Many patterns in ordinary unconsciousness, on the other hand, can simply be dropped once you know that you don't want them and don't need them anymore, once you realize that you have a choice, that you are not just a bundle of conditioned reflexes. All this implies that you are able to access the power of Now. Without it, you have no choice.

If you call some emotions negative, aren't you creating a mental polarity of good and bad, as you explained earlier?

No. The polarity was created at an earlier stage when your mind judged the present moment as bad; this judgment then created the negative emotion.

But if you call some emotions negative, aren't you really saying that they shouldn't be there, that it's not okay to have those emotions? My understanding is that we should give ourselves permission to have whatever feelings come up, rather than judge them as bad or say that we shouldn't have them. It's okay to feel resentful; it's okay to be angry, irritated, moody, or whatever — otherwise, we get into repression, inner conflict, or denial. Everything is okay as it is.

Of course. Once a mind pattern, an emotion or a reaction is there, accept it. You were not conscious enough to have a choice in the matter. That's not a judgment, just a fact. If you *had* a choice, or realized that you *do* have a choice, would you choose suffering or joy, ease or unease, peace or conflict? Would you choose a thought or feeling that cuts you off from your natural state of well-being, the joy of life within? Any such feeling I call negative, which simply means bad. Not in the sense that "You shouldn't have done that" but just plain factual bad, like feeling sick in the stomach.

How is it possible that humans killed in excess of 100 million fellow humans in the twentieth century alone?[4] Humans inflicting pain of such magnitude on one another is beyond anything you can imagine. And that's not taking into account the mental, emotional and physical violence, the torture, pain, and cruelty they continue to inflict on each other as well as on other sentient beings on a daily basis.

Do they act in this way because they are in touch with their natural state, the joy of life within? Of course not. Only people who are in a deeply negative state, who feel very bad indeed, would create such a reality as a reflection of how they feel. Now they are engaged in destroying nature and the planet that sustains them. Unbelievable but true. Humans are a dangerously insane and very sick species. That's not a judgment. It's a fact. It is also a fact that the sanity *is* there underneath the madness. Healing and redemption are available right now.

Coming back specifically to what you said — it is certainly true that, when you accept your resentment, moodiness, anger, and so on, you are no longer forced to act them out blindly, and you are less likely to project them onto others. But I wonder if you are not deceiving yourself. When you have been practicing acceptance for a while, as you have, there comes a point when you need to go on to the next stage, where those negative emotions are not created anymore. If you don't, your "acceptance" just becomes a mental label that allows your ego to continue to indulge in unhappiness and so strengthen its sense of separation from other people, your surroundings, your here and now. As you know, separation is the basis for the ego's sense of identity. True acceptance would transmute those feelings at once. And if you really knew deeply that everything is "okay," as you put it, and which of course is true, then would you have those negative feelings in the first place? Without judgment, without resistance to what *is*, they would not arise. You have an idea in your mind that "everything is okay," but deep down you don't really believe it, and so the old mental-emotional patterns of resistance are still in place. That's what makes you feel bad.

That's okay, too.

Are you defending your right to be unconscious, your right to suffer? Don't worry: nobody is going to take that away from you. Once you realize that a certain kind of food makes you sick, would you carry on eating that food and keep asserting that it is okay to be sick?

WHEREVER YOU ARE, BE THERE TOTALLY

Can you give some more examples of ordinary unconsciousness?

See if you can catch yourself complaining, in either speech or thought, about a situation you find yourself in, what other people do or say, your surroundings, your life situation, even the weather. To complain is always nonacceptance of what *is*. It invariably carries an unconscious negative charge. When you complain, you make yourself into a victim. When you speak out, you are in your power. So change the situation by taking action or by speaking out if necessary or possible; leave the situation or accept it. All else is madness.

Ordinary unconsciousness is always linked in some way with denial of the Now. The Now, of course, also implies the here. Are you resisting your here and now? Some people would always rather be somewhere else. Their "here" is never good enough. Through self-observation, find out if that is the case in your life. Wherever you are, be there totally. If you find your here and now intolerable and it makes you unhappy, you have three options: remove yourself from the situation, change it, or accept it totally. If you want to take responsibility for your life, you must choose one of those three options, and you must choose now. Then accept the consequences. No excuses. No negativity. No psychic pollution. Keep your inner space clear.

If you take any action — leaving or changing your situation — drop the negativity first, if at all possible. Action arising out of insight into what is required is more effective than action arising out of negativity.

Any action is often better than no action, especially if you have been stuck in an unhappy situation for a long time. If it is a mistake, at least you learn something, in which case it's no longer a mistake. If you remain stuck, you learn nothing. Is fear preventing you from taking action? Acknowledge the fear, watch it, take your attention into it, be fully present with it. Doing so cuts the link between the fear and your thinking. *Don't let the fear rise up into your mind.* Use the power of the Now. Fear cannot prevail against it.

If there is truly nothing that you can do to change your here and now, and you can't remove yourself from the situation, then accept your here and now totally by dropping all inner resistance. The false, unhappy self that loves feeling miserable, resentful, or sorry for itself can then no longer survive. This is called surrender. Surrender is not weakness. There is great strength in it. Only a surrendered person has spiritual power. Through surrender, you will be free internally of the situation. You may then find that the situation changes without any effort on your part. In any case, you are free.

Or is there something that you "should" be doing but are not doing it? Get up and do it now. Alternatively, completely accept your inactivity, laziness, or passivity at this moment, if that is your choice. Go into it fully. Enjoy it. Be as lazy or inactive as you can. If you go into it fully and consciously, you will soon come out of it. Or maybe you won't. Either way, there is no inner conflict, no resistance, no negativity.

Are you stressed? Are you so busy getting to the future that the present is reduced to a means of getting there? Stress is caused by being "here" but wanting to be "there," or being in the present but wanting to be in the future. It's a split that tears you apart inside. To create and live with such an inner split is insane. The fact that everyone else is doing it doesn't make it any less insane. If you have to, you can move fast, work fast, or even run, without projecting yourself into the future and without resisting the present. As you move, work, run — do it totally. Enjoy the flow of energy, the high energy of that moment. Now you are no longer stressed, no longer splitting yourself in two. Just moving, running, working — and enjoying it. Or you can drop the whole thing and sit on a park bench. But when you do, watch your mind. It may say: "You should be working. You are wasting time." Observe the mind. Smile at it.

Does the past take up a great deal of your attention? Do you frequently talk and think about it, either positively or negatively? The great things that you have achieved, your adventures or experiences, or your victim story and the dreadful things that were done to you, or maybe what you did to someone else? Are your thought processes creating guilt, pride, resentment, anger, regret, or self-pity? Then you are not only reinforcing a false sense of self but also helping to accelerate your body's aging process by creating an accumulation of past in your psyche. Verify this for yourself by observing those around you who have a strong tendency to hold on to the past.

Die to the past every moment. You don't need it. Only refer to it when it is absolutely relevant to the present. Feel the power of this moment and the fullness of Being. Feel your presence.

Are you worried? Do you have many "what if" thoughts? You are identified with your mind, which is projecting itself into an imaginary future situation and creating fear. There is no way that you can cope with such a situation, because it doesn't exist. It's a mental phantom. You can stop this health- and life-corroding insanity simply by acknowledging the present moment. Become aware of your breathing. Feel the air flowing in and out of your body. Feel your inner energy field. All that you ever have to deal with, cope with, in real life — as opposed to imaginary mind projections — is *this moment*. Ask yourself what "problem" you have right now, not next year, tomorrow, or five minutes from now. What is wrong with this moment? You can always cope with the Now, but you can never cope with the future —

nor do you have to. The answer, the strength, the right action or the resource will be there when you need it, not before, not after.

"One day I'll make it." Is your goal taking up so much of your attention that you reduce the present moment to a means to an end? Is it taking the joy out of your doing? Are you waiting to start living? If you develop such a mind pattern, no matter what you achieve or get, the present will never be good enough; the future will always seem better. A perfect recipe for permanent dissatisfaction and non-fulfillment, don't you agree?

Are you a habitual "waiter"? How much of your life do you spend waiting? What I call "small-scale waiting" is waiting in line at the post office, in a traffic jam, at the airport, or waiting for someone to arrive, to finish work, and so on. "Large-scale waiting" is waiting for the next vacation, for a better job, for the children to grow up, for a truly meaningful relationship, for success, to make money, to be important, to become enlightened. It is not uncommon for people to spend their whole life waiting to start living.

Waiting is a state of mind. Basically, it means that you want the future; you don't want the present. You don't want what you've got, and you want what you haven't got. With every kind of waiting, you unconsciously create inner conflict between your here and now, where you don't want to be, and the projected future, where you want to be. This greatly reduces the quality of your life by making you lose the present.

There is nothing wrong with striving to improve your life situation. You can improve your life situation, but you cannot improve your life. Life is primary. Life is your deepest inner Being. It is already whole, complete, perfect. Your life situation consists of your circumstances and your experiences. There is nothing wrong with setting goals and striving to achieve things. The mistake lies in using it as a substitute for the feeling of life, for Being. The only point of access for that is the Now. You are then like an architect who pays no attention to the foundation of a building but spends a lot of time working on the superstructure.

For example, many people are waiting for prosperity. It cannot come in the future. When you honor, acknowledge, and fully accept your present reality — where you are, who you are, what you are doing right now — when you fully accept what you have got, you are grateful for what you have got, grateful for what *is*, grateful for Being. Gratitude for the present moment and the fullness of *life now* is true prosperity. It cannot come in the future. Then, in time, that prosperity manifests for you in various ways.

If you are dissatisfied with what you have got, or even frustrated or angry about your present lack, that may motivate you to become rich, but even if you do make millions, you will continue to experience the inner condition of lack, and deep down you will continue to feel unfulfilled. You may have many exciting experiences that money can buy, but they will come and go and always leave you with an empty feeling and the need for further physical or psychological gratification. You won't abide in Being and so feel the fullness of life now that alone is true prosperity.

So give up waiting as a state of mind. When you catch yourself slipping into waiting...snap out of it. Come into the present moment. Just be, and enjoy being. If you are present, there is never any need for you to wait for anything. So next time somebody says, "Sorry to have kept you waiting," you can reply, "That's all right, I wasn't waiting. I was just standing here enjoying myself — in joy in my self."

These are just a few of the habitual mind strategies for denying the present moment that are part of ordinary unconsciousness. They are easy to overlook because they are so much a part of normal living: the background static of perpetual discontent. But the more you practice monitoring your inner mental-emotional state, the easier it will be to know when you have been trapped in past or future, which is to say unconscious, and to awaken out of the dream of time into the present. But beware: The false, unhappy self, based on mind identification, lives on time. It knows that the present moment is its own death and so feels very threatened by it. It will do all it can to take you out of it. It will try to keep you trapped in time.

THE INNER PURPOSE OF YOUR LIFE'S JOURNEY

I can see the truth of what you are saying, but I still think that we must have purpose on our life's journey; otherwise we just drift, and purpose means future, doesn't it? How do we reconcile that with living in the present?

When you are on a journey, it is certainly helpful to know where you are going or at least the general direction in which you are moving, but don't forget: the only thing that is ultimately real about your journey is the step that you are taking at this moment. That's all there ever is.

Your life's journey has an outer purpose and an inner purpose. The outer purpose is to arrive at your goal or destination, to accomplish what you set out to do, to achieve this or that, which, of course, implies future. But if your destination, or the steps you are going to take in the future, take up so much of your attention that they become more important to you than the step you are taking now, then you completely miss the journey's inner purpose, which has nothing to do with *where* you are going or *what* you are doing, but everything to do with *how*. It has nothing to do with future but everything to do with the quality of your consciousness at this moment. The outer purpose belongs to the horizontal dimension of space and time; the inner purpose concerns a deepening of your Being in the vertical dimension of the timeless Now. Your outer journey may contain a million steps; your inner journey only has one: the step you are taking right now. As you become more deeply aware of this one step, you realize that it already contains within itself all the other steps as well as the destination. This one step then becomes transformed into an expression of perfection, an act of great beauty and quality. It will have taken you into Being, and the light of Being will shine through it. This is both the purpose and the fulfillment of your inner journey, the journey into yourself.

∫

Does it matter whether we achieve our outer purpose, whether we suc-
ceed or fail in the world?

It will matter to you as long as you haven't realized your inner purpose. After that, the outer purpose is just a game that you may continue to play simply because you enjoy it. It is also possible to fail
completely in your outer purpose and at the same time totally succeed
in your inner purpose. Or the other way around, which is actually
more common: outer riches and inner poverty, or to "gain the world
and lose your soul," as Jesus puts it. Ultimately, of course, *every* outer
purpose is doomed to "fail" sooner or later, simply because it is subject to the law of impermanence of all things. The sooner you realize
that your outer purpose cannot give you lasting fulfillment, the better.
When you have seen the limitations of your outer purpose, you give
up your unrealistic expectation that it should make you happy, and
you make it subservient to your inner purpose.

THE PAST CANNOT SURVIVE IN YOUR PRESENCE

You mentioned that thinking or talking about the past unnecessarily is
one of the ways in which we avoid the present. But apart from the past
that we remember and perhaps identify with, isn't there another level
of past within us that is much more deep-seated? I am talking about
the unconscious past that conditions our lives, especially through early
childhood experiences, perhaps even past-life experiences. And then
there is our cultural conditioning, which has to do with where we live
geographically and the historical time period in which we live. All these
things determine how we see the world, how we react, what we think,
what kind of relationships we have, how we live our lives. How could

we ever become conscious of all that or get rid of it? How long would that take? And even if we did, what would there be left?

What is left when illusion ends?

There is no need to investigate the unconscious past in you except as it manifests at this moment as a thought, an emotion, a desire, a reaction, or an external event that happens to you. Whatever you need to know about the unconscious past in you, the challenges of the present will bring it out. If you delve into the past, it will become a bottomless pit: There is always more. You may think that you need more time to understand the past or become free of it, in other words, that the future will eventually free you of the past. This is a delusion. Only the present can free you of the past. More time cannot free you of time. Access the power of Now. That is the key.

What is the power of Now?

None other than the power of your presence, your consciousness liberated from thought forms.

So deal with the past on the level of the present. The more attention you give to the past, the more you energize it, and the more likely you are to make a "self" out of it. Don't misunderstand: Attention is essential, but not to the past as past. Give attention to the present; give attention to your behavior, to your reactions, moods, thoughts, emotions, fears, and desires as they occur in the present. *There's* the past in you. If you can be present enough to watch all those things, not critically or analytically but nonjudgmentally, then you are dealing with the past and dissolving it through the power of your presence. You cannot find yourself by going into the past. You find yourself by coming into the present.

Isn't it helpful to understand the past and so understand why we do certain things, react in certain ways, or why we unconsciously create our particular kind of drama, patterns in relationships, and so on?

75

As you become more conscious of your present reality, you may suddenly get certain insights as to *why* your conditioning functions in those particular ways; for example, why your relationships follow certain patterns, and you may remember things that happened in the past or see them more clearly. That is fine and can be helpful, but it is not essential. What is essential is your conscious presence. *That* dissolves the past. That is the transformative agent. So don't seek to understand the past, but be as present as you can. The past cannot survive in your presence. It can only survive in your absence.

CHAPTER FIVE

THE STATE OF PRESENCE

IT'S NOT WHAT YOU THINK IT IS

You keep talking about the state of presence as the key. I think I understand it intellectually, but I don't know if I have ever truly experienced it. I wonder — is it what I think it is, or is it something entirely different?

It's not what you think it is! You can't think about presence, and the mind can't understand it. Understanding presence is *being* present.

Try a little experiment. Close your eyes and say to yourself: "I wonder what my next thought is going to be." Then become very alert and wait for the next thought. Be like a cat watching a mouse hole. What thought is going to come out of the mouse hole? Try it now.

Well?

I had to wait for quite a long time before a thought came in.

Exactly. As long as you are in a state of intense presence, you are free of thought. You are still, yet highly alert. The instant your conscious attention sinks below a certain level, thought rushes in. The mental noise returns; the stillness is lost. You are back in time.

To test their degree of presence, some Zen masters have been known to creep up on their students from behind and suddenly hit them with a stick. Quite a shock! If the student had been fully present and in a state of alertness, if he had "kept his loin girded and his lamp burning," which is one of the analogies that Jesus uses for presence, he would have noticed the master coming up from behind and stopped him or stepped aside. But if he were hit, that would mean he was immersed in thought, which is to say absent, unconscious.

To stay present in everyday life, it helps to be deeply rooted within yourself; otherwise, the mind, which has incredible momentum, will drag you along like a wild river.

What do you mean by "rooted within yourself"?

It means to inhabit your body fully. To always have some of your attention in the inner energy field of your body. To feel the body from within, so to speak. Body awareness keeps you present. It anchors you in the Now (see Chapter 6).

THE ESOTERIC MEANING OF "WAITING"

In a sense, the state of presence could be compared to waiting. Jesus used the analogy of waiting in some of his parables. This is not the usual bored or restless kind of waiting that is a denial of the present and that I spoke about already. It is not a waiting in which your attention is focused on some point in the future and the present is perceived as an undesirable obstacle that prevents you from having what you want. There is a qualitatively different kind of waiting, one that requires your total alertness. Something could happen at any moment, and if you are not absolutely awake, absolutely still, you will miss it. This is the kind of waiting Jesus talks about. In that state, all your attention is in the Now. There is none left for daydreaming, thinking, remembering, anticipating. There is no tension in it, no fear, just alert presence. You are present with your whole Being, with every cell of your body. In that state, the "you" that has a past and a future, the personality if you like, is hardly there anymore. And yet nothing of value is lost. You are still essentially yourself. In fact, you are more fully yourself than you ever were before, or rather it is only *now* that you are truly yourself.

"Be like a servant waiting for the return of the master," says Jesus. The servant does not know at what hour the master is going to come. So he stays awake, alert, poised, still, lest he miss the master's arrival. In another parable, Jesus speaks of the five careless (unconscious) women who do not have enough oil (consciousness) to keep their lamps burning (stay present) and so miss the bridegroom (the Now) and don't get to the wedding feast (enlightenment). These five stand in contrast to the five wise women who have enough oil (stay conscious).

Even the men who wrote the Gospels did not understand the meaning of these parables, so the first misinterpretations and distortions crept in as they were written down. With subsequent erroneous interpretations, the real meaning was completely lost. These are parables not about the end of the world but about the end of psychological time. They point to the transcendence of the egoic mind and the possibility of living in an entirely new state of consciousness.

BEAUTY ARISES IN THE STILLNESS OF YOUR PRESENCE

What you have just described is something that I occasionally experience for brief moments when I am alone and surrounded by nature.

Yes. Zen masters use the word *satori* to describe a flash of insight, a moment of no-mind and total presence. Although *satori* is not a lasting transformation, be grateful when it comes, for it gives you a taste of enlightenment. You may, indeed, have experienced it many times without knowing what it is and realizing its importance. Presence is needed to become aware of the beauty, the majesty, the sacredness of nature. Have you ever gazed up into the infinity of space on a clear night, awestruck by the absolute stillness and inconceivable vastness of it? Have you listened, truly listened, to the sound of a mountain stream in the forest? Or to the song of a blackbird at dusk on a quiet summer evening? To become aware of such things, the mind needs to be still. You have to put down for a moment your personal baggage of problems, of past and future, as well as all your knowledge; otherwise, you will see but not see, hear but not hear. Your total presence is required.

Beyond the beauty of the external forms, there is more here: something that cannot be named, something ineffable, some deep, inner, holy essence. Whenever and wherever there is beauty, this inner essence shines through somehow. It only reveals itself to you when you are present. Could it be that this nameless essence and your presence are one and the same? Would it be there without your presence? Go deeply into it. Find out for yourself.

When you experienced those moments of presence, you likely didn't realize that you were briefly in a state of no-mind. This is because the gap between that state and the influx of thought was too narrow. Your *satori* may only have lasted for a few seconds before the mind came in, but it was there; otherwise, you would not have experienced the beauty. Mind can neither recognize nor create beauty. Only for a few seconds, while you were completely present, was that beauty or that sacredness there. Because of the narrowness of that gap and a lack of vigilance and alertness on your part, you were probably unable to see the fundamental difference between the perception, the thought-less awareness of beauty, and the naming and interpreting of it as thought: The time gap was so small that it seemed to be a single process. The truth is, however, that the moment thought came in, all you had was a memory of it.

The wider the time gap between perception and thought, the

more depth there is to you as a human being, which is to say the more conscious you are.

Many people are so imprisoned in their minds that the beauty of nature does not really exist for them. They might say, "What a pretty flower," but that's just a mechanical mental labeling. Because they are not still, not present, they don't truly see the flower, don't feel its essence, its holiness — just as they don't know themselves, don't feel their own essence, their own holiness.

Because we live in such a mind-dominated culture, most modern art, architecture, music, and literature are devoid of beauty, of inner essence, with very few exceptions. The reason is that the people who create those things cannot — even for a moment — free themselves from their mind. So they are never in touch with that place within where true creativity and beauty arise. The mind left to itself creates monstrosities, and not only in art galleries. Look at our urban landscapes and industrial wastelands. No civilization has ever produced so much ugliness.

REALIZING PURE CONSCIOUSNESS

Is presence the same as Being?

When you become conscious of Being, what is really happening is that Being becomes conscious of itself. When Being becomes conscious of itself — that's presence. Since Being, consciousness, and life are synonymous, we could say that presence means consciousness becoming conscious of itself, or life attaining self-consciousness. But don't get attached to the words, and don't make an effort to understand this. There is nothing that you need to understand before you can become present.

I do understand what you just said, but it seems to imply that Being, the ultimate transcendental reality, is not yet complete, that it is undergoing a process of development. Does God need time for personal growth?

Yes, but only as seen from the limited perspective of the manifested universe. In the Bible, God declares: "I am the Alpha and the Omega, and I am the living One." In the timeless realm where God dwells, which is also *your* home, the beginning and the end, the Alpha and the Omega, are one, and the essence of everything that ever has been and ever will be is eternally present in an unmanifested state of oneness and perfection — totally beyond anything the human mind can ever imagine or comprehend. In our world of seemingly separate forms, however, timeless perfection is an inconceivable concept. Here even consciousness, which is the light emanating from the eternal Source, seems to be subject to a process of development, but this is due to our limited perception. It is not so in absolute terms. Nevertheless, let me continue to speak for a moment about the evolution of consciousness in this world.

Everything that exists has Being, has God-essence, has some degree of consciousness. Even a stone has rudimentary consciousness; otherwise, it would not be, and its atoms and molecules would disperse. Everything is alive. The sun, the earth, plants, animals, humans — all are expressions of consciousness in varying degrees, consciousness manifesting as form.

The world arises when consciousness takes on shapes and forms, thought forms and material forms. Look at the millions of life forms on this planet alone. In the sea, on land, in the air — and then each life form is replicated millions of times. To what end? Is someone or something playing a game, a game with form? This is what the ancient seers of India asked themselves. They saw the world as *lila*, a kind of divine game that God is playing. The individual life forms are obviously not very important in this game. In the sea, most life forms don't survive for more than a few minutes after being born. The human form turns to dust pretty quickly too, and when it is gone it is as if it had never been. Is that tragic or cruel? Only if you create a separate identity for each form, if you forget that its consciousness is God-essence expressing itself in form. But you don't truly *know* that until you realize your own God-essence as pure consciousness.

If a fish is born in your aquarium and you call it John, write out a birth certificate, tell him about his family history, and two minutes later he gets eaten by another fish — that's tragic. But it's only tragic because you projected a separate self where there was none. You got hold of a fraction of a dynamic process, a molecular dance, and made a separate entity out of it.

Consciousness takes on the disguise of forms until they reach such complexity that it completely loses itself in them. In present-day humans, consciousness is completely identified with its disguise. It only knows itself as form and therefore lives in fear of the annihilation of its physical or psychological form. This is the egoic mind, and this is where considerable dysfunction sets in. It now looks as if something had gone very wrong somewhere along the line of evolution. But even this is part of *lila*, the divine game. Finally, the pressure of suffering created by this apparent dysfunction forces consciousness to disidentify from form and awakens it from its dream of form: It regains self-consciousness, but it is at a far deeper level than when it lost it.

This process is explained by Jesus in his parable of the lost son, who leaves his father's home, squanders his wealth, becomes destitute, and is then forced by his suffering to return home. When he does, his father *loves him more* than before. The son's state is the same as it was before, yet not the same. It has an added dimension of depth. The parable describes a journey from unconscious perfection, through apparent imperfection and "evil" to conscious perfection.

Can you now see the deeper and wider significance of becoming present as the watcher of your mind? Whenever you watch the mind, you withdraw consciousness from mind forms, which then becomes what we call the watcher or the witness. Consequently, the watcher — pure consciousness beyond form — becomes stronger, and the mental formations become weaker. When we talk about watching the mind we are personalizing an event that is truly of cosmic significance: through you, consciousness is awakening out of its dream of identification with form and withdrawing from form. This foreshadows, but is already part of, an event that is probably still in the distant future as far as chronological time is concerned. The event is called — the end of the world.

When consciousness frees itself from its identification with physical and mental forms, it becomes what we may call pure or enlightened consciousness, or presence. This has already happened in a few individuals, and it seems destined to happen soon on a much larger scale, although there is no absolute guarantee that it *will* happen. Most humans are still in the grip of the egoic mode of consciousness: identified with their mind and run by their mind. If they do not free themselves from their mind in time, they will be destroyed by it. They will experience increasing confusion, conflict, violence, illness, despair, madness. Egoic mind has become like a sinking ship. If you don't get off, you will go down with it. The collective egoic mind is the most dangerously insane and destructive entity ever to inhabit this planet. What do you think will happen on this planet if human consciousness remains unchanged?

Already for most humans, the only respite they find from their own minds is to occasionally revert to a level of consciousness below thought. Everyone does that every night during sleep. But this also happens to some extent through sex, alcohol, and other drugs that suppress excessive mind activity. If it weren't for alcohol, tranquilizers, antidepressants, as well as the illegal drugs, which are all consumed in vast quantities, the insanity of the human mind would become even more glaringly obvious than it is already. I believe that, if deprived of their drugs, a large part of the population would become a danger to themselves and others. These drugs, of course, simply keep you stuck in dysfunction. Their widespread use only delays the breakdown of the old mind structures and the emergence of higher consciousness. While individual users may get some relief from the daily torture inflicted on them by their minds, they are prevented from generating enough conscious presence to rise above thought and so find true liberation.

Falling back to a level of consciousness below mind, which is the pre-thinking level of our distant ancestors and of animals and plants, is not an option for us. There is no way back. If the human race is to survive, it will have to go on to the next stage. Consciousness is evolving throughout the universe in billions of forms. So even if we didn't make it, this wouldn't matter on a cosmic scale. No gain in consciousness is ever lost, so it would simply express itself through some other form. But the very fact that I am speaking here and you are listening or reading this is a clear sign that the new consciousness *is* gaining a foothold on the planet.

There is nothing personal in this: I am not teaching you. You are consciousness, and you are listening to yourself. There is an Eastern saying: "The teacher and the taught together create the teaching." In any case, the words in themselves are not important. They are not the Truth; they only point to it. I speak from presence, and as I speak, you may be able to join me in that state. Although every word that I use has a history, of course, and comes from the past, as all language does, the words that I speak to you now are carriers of the high-energy frequency of presence, quite apart from the meaning they convey as words.

Silence is an even more potent carrier of presence, so when you read this or listen to me speak, be aware of the silence between and underneath the words. Be aware of the gaps. To listen to the silence, wherever you are, is an easy and direct way of becoming present. Even if there is noise, there is always some silence underneath and in between the sounds. Listening to the silence immediately creates stillness inside you. Only the stillness in you can perceive the silence outside. And what is stillness other than presence, consciousness freed from thought forms? Here is the living realization of what we have been talking about.

∫

CHRIST: THE REALITY OF YOUR DIVINE PRESENCE

Don't get attached to any one word. You can substitute "Christ" for presence, if that is more meaningful to you. Christ is your God-essence or the Self, as it is sometimes called in the East. The only difference between Christ and presence is that Christ refers to your indwelling divinity regardless of whether you are conscious of it or not, whereas presence means your *awakened* divinity or God-essence.

Many misunderstandings and false beliefs about Christ will clear if you realize that there is no past or future in Christ. To say that Christ *was* or *will be* is a contradiction in terms. Jesus was. He was a man who lived two thousand years ago and realized divine presence, his true nature. And so he said: "Before Abraham was, I am." He did not say: "I already existed before Abraham was born." That would have meant that he was still within the dimension of time and form identity. The words *I am* used in a sentence that starts in the past tense indicate a radical shift, a discontinuity in the temporal dimension. It is a Zen-like statement of great profundity. Jesus attempted to convey directly, not through discursive thought, the meaning of presence, of self-realization. He had gone beyond the consciousness dimension governed by time, into the realm of the timeless. The dimension of eternity had come into this world. Eternity, of course, does not mean endless time, but no time. Thus, the man Jesus became Christ, a vehicle for pure consciousness. And what is God's self-definition in the Bible? Did God say "I have always been, and I always will be?" Of course not. That would have given reality to past and future. God said: "I AM THAT I AM." No time here, just presence.

The "second coming" of Christ is a transformation of human consciousness, a shift from time to presence, from thinking to pure consciousness, not the arrival of some man or woman. If "Christ" were to return tomorrow in some externalized form, what could he or she possibly say to you other than this: "I am the Truth. I am divine presence. I am eternal life. I am within you. I am here. I am Now."

Never personalize Christ. Don't make Christ into a form identity. Avatars, divine mothers, enlightened masters, the very few that are real, are not special as persons. Without a false self to uphold, defend, and feed, they are more simple, more ordinary than the ordinary man or woman. Anyone with a strong ego would regard them as insignificant or, more likely, not see them at all.

If you are drawn to an enlightened teacher, it is because there is already enough presence in you to recognize presence in another. There were many people who did not recognize Jesus or the Buddha, as there are and always have been many people who are drawn to false teachers. Egos are drawn to bigger egos. Darkness cannot recognize light. Only light can recognize light. So don't believe that the light is outside you or that it can only come through one particular form. If only your master is an incarnation of God, then who are you? Any kind of exclusivity is identification with form, and identification with form means ego, no matter how well disguised.

Use the master's presence to reflect your own identity beyond name and form back to you and to become more intensely present yourself. You will soon realize that there is no "mine" or "yours" in presence. Presence is one.

Group work can also be helpful for intensifying the light of your presence. A group of people coming together in a state of presence generates a collective energy field of great intensity. It not only raises the degree of presence of each member of the group but also helps to free the collective human consciousness from its current state of mind dominance. This will make the state of presence increasingly more accessible to individuals. However, unless at least one member of the group is already firmly established in it and thus can hold the energy frequency of that state, the egoic mind can easily reassert itself and sabotage the group's endeavors. Although group work is invaluable, it is not enough, and you must not come to depend on it. Nor must you come to depend on a teacher or a master, except during the transitional period, when you are learning the meaning and practice of presence.

CHAPTER SIX

THE INNER BODY

BEING IS YOUR DEEPEST SELF

You spoke earlier about the importance of having deep roots within or inhabiting the body. Can you explain what you meant by that?

The body can become a point of access into the realm of Being. Let's go into that more deeply now.

I am still not quite sure if I fully understand what you mean by Being.

"Water? What do you mean by that? I don't understand it." This is what a fish would say if it had a human mind.

Please stop trying to understand Being. You have already had significant glimpses of Being, but the mind will always try to squeeze it into a little box and then put a label on it. It cannot be done. It cannot become an object of knowledge. In Being, subject and object merge into one.

Being can be *felt* as the ever-present *I am* that is beyond name and form. To feel and thus to know that you *are* and to abide in that deeply rooted state is enlightenment, is the truth that Jesus says will make you free.

Free from what?

Free from the *illusion* that you are nothing more than your physical body and your mind. This "illusion of the self," as the Buddha calls it, is the core error. Free from *fear* in its countless disguises as the inevitable consequence of that illusion — the fear that is your constant tormentor as long as you derive your sense of self only from this ephemeral and vulnerable form. And free from *sin*, which is the suffering you unconsciously inflict on yourself and others as long as this illusory sense of self governs what you think, say, and do.

LOOK BEYOND THE WORDS

I don't like the word sin. *It implies that I am being judged and found guilty.*

I can understand that. Over the centuries, many erroneous views and interpretations have accumulated around words such as *sin*, due to ignorance, misunderstanding, or a desire to control, but they contain an essential core of truth. If you are unable to look beyond such interpretations and so cannot recognize the reality to which the word points, then don't use it. Don't get stuck on the level of words. A word is no more than a means to an end. It's an abstraction. Not unlike a signpost, it points beyond itself. The word *honey* isn't honey. You can study and talk about honey for as long as you like, but you won't really *know* it until you taste it. After you have tasted it, the word becomes less important to you. You won't be attached to it anymore. Similarly, you can talk or think about *God* continuously for the rest of your life, but does that mean you know or have even glimpsed the reality to which the word points? It really is no more than an obsessive attachment to a signpost, a mental idol.

The reverse also applies: If, for whatever reason, you disliked the word *honey*, that might prevent you from ever tasting it. If you had a strong aversion to the word *God*, which is a negative form of attachment, you may be denying not just the word but also the reality to which it points. You would be cutting yourself off from the possibility of experiencing that reality. All this is, of course, intrinsically connected with being identified with your mind.

So, if a word doesn't work for you anymore, then drop it and replace it with one that does work. If you don't like the word *sin*, then call it unconsciousness or insanity. That may get you closer to the truth, the reality behind the word, than a long-misused word like *sin*, and leaves little room for guilt.

I don't like those words either. They imply that there is something wrong with me. I am being judged.

Of course there is something wrong with you — and you are not being judged.

I don't mean to offend you personally, but do you not belong to the human race that has killed over 100 million members of their own species in the twentieth century alone?

You mean guilt by association?

It is not a question of guilt. But as long as you are run by the egoic mind, you are part of the collective insanity. Perhaps you haven't looked very deeply into the human condition in its state of dominance by the egoic mind. Open your eyes and see the fear, the despair, the greed, and the violence that are all-pervasive. See the heinous cruelty and suffering on an unimaginable scale that humans have inflicted and continue to inflict on each other as well as on other life forms on the planet. You don't need to condemn. Just observe. That is sin. That is insanity. That is unconsciousness. Above all, don't forget to observe your own mind. Seek out the root of the insanity there.

FINDING YOUR INVISIBLE AND INDESTRUCTIBLE REALITY

You said that identification with our physical form is part of the illusion, so how can the body, the physical form, bring you to a realization of Being?

91

The body that you can see and touch cannot take you into Being. But that visible and tangible body is only an outer shell, or rather a limited and distorted perception of a deeper reality. In your natural state of connectedness with Being, this deeper reality can be felt every moment as the invisible inner body, the animating presence within you. So to "inhabit the body" is to feel the body from within, to feel the life inside the body and thereby come to know that you are beyond the outer form.

But that is only the beginning of an inward journey that will take you ever more deeply into a realm of great stillness and peace, yet also of great power and vibrant life. At first, you may only get fleeting glimpses of it, but through them you will begin to realize that you are not just a meaningless fragment in an alien universe, briefly suspended between birth and death, allowed a few short-lived pleasures followed by pain and ultimate annihilation. Underneath your outer form, you are connected with something so vast, so immeasurable and sacred, that it cannot be conceived or spoken of — yet I am speaking of it now. I am speaking of it not to give you something to believe in but to show you how you can know it for yourself.

You are cut off from Being as long as your mind takes up all your attention. When this happens — and it happens continuously for most people — you are not in your body. The mind absorbs all your consciousness and transforms it into mind stuff. You cannot stop thinking. Compulsive thinking has become a collective disease. Your whole sense of who you are is then derived from mind activity. Your identity, as it is no longer rooted in Being, becomes a vulnerable and ever-needy mental construct, which creates fear as the predominant underlying emotion. The one thing that truly matters is then missing from your life: awareness of your deeper self — your invisible and indestructible reality.

To become conscious of Being, you need to reclaim consciousness from the mind. This is one of the most essential tasks on your spiritual journey. It will free vast amounts of consciousness that previously had been trapped in useless and compulsive thinking. A very effective way of doing this is simply to take the focus of your attention away from thinking and direct it into the body, where Being can be felt in the first instance as the invisible energy field that gives life to what you perceive as the physical body.

CONNECTING WITH THE INNER BODY

Please try it now. You may find it helpful to close your eyes for this practice. Later on, when "being in the body" has become natural and easy, this will no longer be necessary. Direct your attention into the body. Feel it from within. Is it alive? Is there life in your hands, arms, legs, and feet — in your abdomen, your chest? Can you feel the subtle energy field that pervades the entire body and gives vibrant life to every organ and every cell? Can you feel it simultaneously in all parts of the body as a single field of energy? Keep focusing on the feeling of your inner body for a few moments. Do not start to think about it. Feel it. The more attention you give it, the clearer and stronger this feeling will become. It will feel as if every cell is becoming more alive, and if you have a strong visual sense, you may get an image of your body becoming luminous. Although such an image can help you temporarily, pay more attention to the feeling than to any image that may arise. An image, no matter how beautiful or powerful, is already defined in form, so there is less scope for penetrating more deeply.

The feeling of your inner body is formless, limitless, and unfathomable. You can always go into it more deeply. If you cannot feel very much at this stage, pay attention to whatever you *can* feel. Perhaps there is just a slight tingling in your hands or feet. That's good enough for the moment. Just focus on the feeling. Your body is coming alive. Later, we will practice some more. Please open your eyes now, but keep some attention in the inner energy field of the body even as you look around the room. The inner body lies at the threshold between your form identity and your essence identity, your true nature. Never lose touch with it.

∫

TRANSFORMATION THROUGH THE BODY

Why have most religions condemned or denied the body? It seems that spiritual seekers have always regarded the body as a hindrance or even as sinful.

Why have so few seekers become finders?

On the level of the body, humans are very close to animals. All the basic bodily functions — pleasure, pain, breathing, eating, drinking, defecating, sleeping, the drive to find a mate and procreate, and of course birth and death — we share with the animals. A long time after their fall from a state of grace and oneness into illusion, humans suddenly woke up in what seemed to be an animal body — and they found this very disturbing. "Don't fool yourself. You are no more than an animal." This seemed to be the truth that was staring them in the face. But it was too disturbing a truth to tolerate. Adam and Eve saw that they were naked, and they became afraid. Unconscious denial of their animal nature set in very quickly. The threat that they might be taken over by powerful instinctual drives and revert back to complete unconsciousness was indeed a very real one. Shame and taboos appeared around certain parts of the body and bodily functions, especially sexuality. The light of their consciousness was not yet strong enough to make friends with their animal nature, to allow it to *be* and even enjoy that aspect of themselves — let alone to go deeply into it to find the divine hidden within it, the reality within the illusion. So they did what they had to do. They began to disassociate from their body. They now saw themselves as *having* a body, rather than just being it.

When religions arose, this disassociation became even more pronounced as the "you are not your body" belief. Countless people in East and West throughout the ages have tried to find God, salvation, or enlightenment through denial of the body. This took the form of denial of sense pleasures and of sexuality in particular, fasting, and other ascetic practices. They even inflicted pain on the body in an attempt to weaken or punish it because they regarded it as sinful. In Christianity, this used to be called mortification of the flesh. Others tried to escape from the body by entering trance states or seeking out-of-the-body experiences. Many still do. Even the Buddha is said to have practiced body denial through fasting and extreme forms of asceticism for six years, but he did not attain enlightenment until after he had given up this practice.

The fact is that no one has ever become enlightened through denying or fighting the body or through an out-of-the-body experience. Although such an experience can be fascinating and can give you a glimpse of the state of liberation from the material form, in the end you will always have to return to the body, where the essential work of transformation takes place. Transformation is *through* the body, not away from it. This is why no true master has ever advocated fighting or leaving the body, although their mind-based followers often have.

Of the ancient teachings concerning the body, only certain fragments survive, such as Jesus's statement that "your whole body will be filled with light," or they survive as myths, such as the belief that Jesus never relinquished his body but remained one with it and ascended into "heaven" with it. Almost no one to this day has understood those fragments or the hidden meaning of certain myths, and the "you are not your body" belief has prevailed universally, leading to body denial and attempts to escape from the body. Countless seekers have thus been prevented from attaining spiritual realization for themselves and becoming finders.

Is it possible to recover the lost teachings on the significance of the body or to reconstruct them from the existing fragments?

There is no need for that. All spiritual teachings originate from the same Source. In that sense, there is and always has been only one master, who manifests in many different forms. I am that master, and so are you, once you are able to access the Source within. And the way to it is through the inner body. Although all spiritual teachings originate from the same Source, once they become verbalized and written down they are obviously no more than collections of words — and a word is nothing but a signpost, as we talked about earlier. All such teachings are signposts pointing the way back to the Source.

I have already spoken of the Truth that is hidden within your body, but I will summarize for you again the lost teachings of the masters — so here is another signpost. Please endeavor to feel your inner body as you read or listen.

SERMON ON THE BODY

What you perceive as a dense physical structure called the body, which is subject to disease, old age, and death, is not ultimately real — is not you. It is a misperception of your essential reality that is beyond birth and death, and is due to the limitations of your mind, which, having lost touch with Being, creates the body as evidence of its illusory belief in separation and to justify its state of fear. But do not turn away from the body, for within that symbol of impermanence, limitation, and death that you perceive as the illusory creation of your mind is concealed the splendor of your essential and immortal reality. Do not turn your attention elsewhere in your search for the Truth, for it is nowhere else to be found but within your body.

Do not fight against the body, for in doing so you are fighting against your own reality. You *are* your body. The body that you can see and touch is only a thin illusory veil. Underneath it lies the invisible inner body, the doorway into Being, into Life Unmanifested.

Through the inner body, you are inseparably connected to this unmanifested One Life — birthless, deathless, eternally present. Through the inner body, you are forever one with God.

∫

HAVE DEEP ROOTS WITHIN

The key is to be in a state of permanent connectedness with your inner body — to feel it at all times. This will rapidly deepen and transform your life. The more consciousness you direct into the inner body, the higher its vibrational frequency becomes, much like a light that grows brighter as you turn up the dimmer switch and so increase the flow of electricity. At this higher energy level, negativity cannot affect you anymore, and you tend to attract new circumstances that reflect this higher frequency.

If you keep your attention in the body as much as possible, you will be anchored in the Now. You won't lose yourself in the external world, and you won't lose yourself in your mind. Thoughts and emotions, fears and desires, may still be there to some extent, but they won't take you over.

Please examine where your attention is at this moment. You are listening to me, or you are reading these words in a book. That is the focus of your attention. You are also peripherally aware of your surroundings, other people, and so on. Furthermore, there may be some mind activity around what you are hearing or reading, some mental commentary. Yet there is no need for any of this to absorb *all* your attention. See if you can be in touch with your inner body at the same time. Keep some of your attention within. Don't let it all flow out. Feel your whole body from within, as a single field of energy. It is almost as if you were listening or reading with your whole body. Let this be your practice in the days and weeks to come.

Do not give all your attention away to the mind and the external world. By all means focus on what you are doing, but feel the inner body at the same time whenever possible. Stay rooted within. Then observe how this changes your state of consciousness and the quality of what you are doing.

Whenever you are waiting, wherever it may be, use that time to feel the inner body. In this way, traffic jams and line-ups become very enjoyable. Instead of mentally projecting yourself away from the Now, go more deeply into the Now by going more deeply into the body.

The art of inner-body awareness will develop into a completely new way of living, a state of permanent connectedness with Being, and will add a depth to your life that you have never known before.

It is easy to stay present as the observer of your mind when you are deeply rooted within your body. No matter what happens on the outside, nothing can shake you anymore.

Unless you stay present — and inhabiting your body is always an essential aspect of it — you will continue to be run by your mind. The script in your head that you learned a long time ago, the conditioning of your mind, will dictate your thinking and your behavior. You may be free of it for brief intervals, but rarely for long. This is especially true when something "goes wrong" or there is some loss or upset. Your conditioned reaction will then be involuntary, automatic, and predictable, fueled by the one basic emotion that underlies the mind-identified state of consciousness: fear.

So when such challenges come, as they always do, make it a habit to go within at once and focus as much as you can on the inner energy field of your body. This need not take long, just a few seconds. But you need to do it the moment that the challenge presents itself. Any delay will allow a conditioned mental-emotional reaction to arise and take you over. When you focus within and feel the inner body, you immediately become still and present as you are withdrawing consciousness from the mind. If a response is required in that situation, it will come up from this deeper level. Just as the sun is infinitely brighter than a candle flame, there is infinitely more intelligence in Being than in your mind.

As long as you are in conscious contact with your inner body, you are like a tree that is deeply rooted in the earth, or a building with a deep and solid foundation. The latter analogy is used by Jesus in the generally misunderstood parable of the two men who build a house. One man builds it on the sand, without a foundation, and when the storms and floods come, the house is swept away. The other man *digs deep* until he reaches the rock, then builds his house, which is not swept away by the floods.

BEFORE YOU ENTER THE BODY, FORGIVE

I felt very uncomfortable when I tried to put my attention on the inner body. There was a feeling of agitation and some nausea. So I haven't been able to experience what you are talking about.

What you felt was a lingering emotion that you were probably unaware of, until you started putting some attention into the body. Unless you first give it some attention, the emotion will prevent you from gaining access to the inner body, which lies at a deeper level underneath it. Attention does not mean that you start *thinking* about it. It means to just observe the emotion, to feel it fully, and so to acknowledge and accept it as it is. Some emotions are easily identified: anger, fear, grief, and so on. Others may be much harder to label. They may just be vague feelings of unease, heaviness, or constriction, halfway between an emotion and a physical sensation. In any case, what matters is not whether you can attach a mental label to it but whether you can bring the feeling of it into awareness as much as possible. Attention is the key to transformation — and full attention also implies acceptance. Attention is like a beam of light — the focused power of your consciousness that transmutes everything into itself.

In a fully functional organism, an emotion has a very short life span. It is like a momentary ripple or wave on the surface of your Being. When you are not in your body, however, an emotion can survive inside you for days or weeks, or join with other emotions of a similar frequency that have merged and become the pain-body, a parasite that can live inside you for years, feed on your energy, lead to physical illness, and make your life miserable (see Chapter 2).

So place your attention on feeling the emotion, and check whether your mind is holding on to a grievance pattern such as blame, self-pity, or resentment that is feeding the emotion. If that is the case, it means that you haven't forgiven. Nonforgiveness is often toward another person or yourself, but it may just as well be toward any situation or condition — past, present or future — that your mind refuses to accept. Yes, there can be nonforgiveness even with regard to the future. This is the mind's refusal to accept uncertainty, to accept that the future is ultimately beyond its control. Forgiveness is to relinquish your grievance and so to let go of grief. It happens naturally once you realize that your grievance serves no purpose except to strengthen a false sense of self. Forgiveness is to offer no resistance to life — to allow life to live through you. The alternatives are pain and suffering, a greatly restricted flow of life energy, and in many cases physical disease.

The moment you truly forgive, you have reclaimed your power from the mind. Nonforgiveness is the very nature of the mind, just as the mind-made false self, the ego, cannot survive without strife and conflict. The mind cannot forgive. Only *you* can. You become present, you enter your body, you feel the vibrant peace and stillness that emanate from Being. That is why Jesus said: "Before you enter the temple, forgive."

YOUR LINK WITH THE UNMANIFESTED

What is the relationship between presence and the inner body?

Presence is pure consciousness — consciousness that has been reclaimed from the mind, from the world of form. The inner body is your link with the Unmanifested, and in its deepest aspect *is* the Unmanifested: the Source from which consciousness emanates as light emanates from the sun. Awareness of the inner body is consciousness remembering its origin and returning to the Source.

Is the Unmanifested the same as Being?

Yes. The word *Unmanifested* attempts, by way of negation, to express That which cannot be spoken, thought or imagined. It points to what it *is* by saying what it is *not*. *Being*, on the other hand, is a positive term. Please don't get attached to either of these words or start believing in them. They are no more than signposts.

You said that presence is consciousness that has been reclaimed from the mind. Who does the reclaiming?

You do. But since in your essence you *are* consciousness, we might as well say that it is an awakening of consciousness from the dream of form. This does not mean that your own form will instantly vanish in an explosion of light. You can continue in your present form yet be aware of the formless and deathless deep within you.

I must admit that this is way beyond my comprehension, and yet on some deeper level I seem to know what you are talking about. It's more like a feeling than anything else. Am I deceiving myself?

No, you are not. Feeling will get you closer to the truth of who you are than thinking. I cannot tell you anything that deep within you don't already know. When you have reached a certain stage of inner connectedness, you recognize the truth when you hear it. If you haven't reached that stage yet, the practice of body awareness will bring about the deepening that is necessary.

SLOWING DOWN THE AGING PROCESS

In the meantime, awareness of the inner body has other benefits in the physical realm. One of them is a significant slowing down of the aging of the physical body.

Whereas the outer body normally appears to grow old and wither fairly quickly, the inner body does not change with time, except that you may feel it more deeply and become it more fully. If you are twenty years old now, the energy field of your inner body will feel just the same when you are eighty. It will be just as vibrantly alive. As soon as your habitual state changes from being out-of-the-body and trapped in your mind to being in-the-body and present in the Now, your physical body will feel lighter, clearer, more alive. As there is more consciousness in the body, its molecular structure actually becomes less dense. More consciousness means a lessening of the illusion of materiality.

When you become identified more with the timeless inner body than with the outer body, when presence becomes your normal mode of consciousness and past and future no longer dominate your attention, you do not accumulate time anymore in your psyche and in the cells of the body. The accumulation of time as the psychological burden of past and future greatly impairs the cells' capacity for self-renewal. So if you inhabit the inner body, the outer body will grow old at a much slower rate, and even when it does, your timeless essence will shine through the outer form, and you will not give the appearance of an old person.

Is there any scientific evidence for this?

Try it out and you will *be* the evidence.

STRENGTHENING THE IMMUNE SYSTEM

Another benefit of this practice in the physical realm is a great strengthening of the immune system which occurs when you inhabit the body. The more consciousness you bring into the body, the stronger the immune system becomes. It is as if every cell awakens and rejoices. The body loves your attention. It is also a potent form of self-healing. Most illnesses creep in when you are not present in the body. If the master is not present in the house, all kinds of shady characters will take up residence there. When you inhabit your body, it will be hard for unwanted guests to enter.

It is not only your physical immune system that becomes strengthened; your psychic immune system is greatly enhanced as well. The latter protects you from the negative mental-emotional force fields of others, which are highly contagious. Inhabiting the body protects you not by putting up a shield, but by raising the frequency vibration of your total energy field, so that anything that vibrates at a lower frequency, such as fear, anger, depression, and so on, now exists in what is virtually a different order of reality. It doesn't enter your field of consciousness anymore, or if it does you don't need to offer any resistance to it because it passes right through you. Please don't just accept or reject what I am saying. Put it to the test.

There is a simple but powerful self-healing meditation that you can do whenever you feel the need to boost your immune system. It is particularly effective if used when you feel the first symptoms of an illness, but it also works with illnesses that are already entrenched if you use it at frequent intervals and with an intense focus. It will also counteract any disruption of your energy field by some form of negativity. However, it is not a substitute for the moment-to-moment practice of being in the body; otherwise, its effect will only be temporary. Here it is.

When you are unoccupied for a few minutes, and especially last thing at night before falling asleep and first thing in the morning before getting up, "flood" your body with consciousness. Close your eyes. Lie flat on your back. Choose different parts of your body to focus your attention on briefly at first: hands, feet, arms, legs, abdomen, chest, head, and so on. Feel the life energy inside those parts as intensely as you can. Stay with each part for fifteen seconds or so. Then let your attention run through the body like a wave a few times, from feet to head and back again. This need only take a minute or so. After that, feel the inner body in its totality, as a single field of energy. Hold that feeling for a few minutes. Be intensely present during that time, present in every cell of your body. Don't be concerned if the mind occasionally succeeds in drawing your attention out of the body and you lose yourself in some thought. As soon as you notice that this has happened, just return your attention to the inner body.

LET THE BREATH TAKE YOU INTO THE BODY

At times, when my mind has been very active, it has acquired such momentum that I find it impossible to take my attention away from it and feel the inner body. This happens particularly when I get into a worry or anxiety pattern. Do you have any suggestions?

If at any time you are finding it hard to get in touch with the inner body, it is usually easier to focus on your breathing first. Conscious breathing, which is a powerful meditation in its own right, will gradually put you in touch with the body. Follow the breath with your attention as it moves in and out of your body. Breathe into the body, and feel your abdomen expanding and contracting slightly with each inhalation and exhalation. If you find it easy to visualize, close your eyes and see yourself surrounded by light or immersed in a luminous substance — a sea of consciousness. Then breathe in that light. Feel that luminous substance filling up your body and making it luminous also. Then gradually focus more on the feeling. You are now in your body. Don't get attached to any visual image.

CREATIVE USE OF MIND

If you need to use your mind for a specific purpose, use it in conjunction with your inner body. Only if you are able to be conscious without thought can you use your mind creatively, and the easiest way to enter that state is through your body. Whenever an answer, a solution, or a creative idea is needed, stop thinking for a moment by focusing attention on your inner energy field. Become aware of the stillness. When you resume thinking, it will be fresh and creative. In any thought activity, make it a habit to go back and forth every few minutes or so between thinking and an inner kind of listening, an inner stillness. We could say: don't just think with your head, think with your whole body.

∫

THE ART OF LISTENING

When listening to another person, don't just listen with your mind, listen with your whole body. Feel the energy field of your inner body as you listen. That takes attention away from thinking and creates a still space that enables you to truly listen without the mind interfering. You are giving the other person space — space to be. It is the most precious gift you can give. Most people don't know how to listen because the major part of their attention is taken up by thinking. They pay more attention to that than to what the other person is saying, and none at all to what really matters: the Being of the other person underneath the words and the mind. Of course, you cannot feel someone else's Being except through your own. This is the beginning of the realization of oneness, which is love. At the deepest level of Being, you are one with all that is.

Most human relationships consist mainly of minds interacting with each other, not of human beings communicating, being in communion. No relationship can thrive in that way, and that is why there is so much conflict in relationships. When the mind is running your life, conflict, strife and problems are inevitable. Being in touch with your inner body creates a clear space of no-mind within which the relationship can flower.

CHAPTER SEVEN

PORTALS INTO THE UNMANIFESTED

GOING DEEPLY INTO THE BODY

I can feel the energy inside my body, especially in my arms and legs, but I don't seem to be able to go more deeply, as you suggested earlier.

Make it into a meditation. It needn't take long. Ten to fifteen minutes of clock time should be sufficient. Make sure first that there are no external distractions such as telephones or people who are likely to interrupt you. Sit on a chair, but don't lean back. Keep the spine erect. Doing so will help you to stay alert. Alternatively, choose your own favorite position for meditation.

Make sure the body is relaxed. Close your eyes. Take a few deep breaths. Feel yourself breathing into the lower abdomen, as it were. Observe how it expands and contracts slightly with each in and out breath. Then become aware of the entire inner energy field of the body. Don't think about it — *feel* it. By doing this, you reclaim consciousness from the mind. If you find it helpful, use the "light" visualization I described earlier.

When you can feel the inner body clearly as a single field of energy, let go, if possible, of any visual image and focus exclusively on the feeling. If you can, also drop any mental image you may still have of the physical body. All that is left then is an all-encompassing sense of presence or "beingness," and the inner body is felt to be without a boundary. Then take your attention even more deeply into that feeling. Become one with it. Merge with the energy field, so that there is no longer a perceived duality of the observer and the observed, of you and your body. The distinction between inner and outer also dissolves now, so there is no inner body anymore. By going deeply into the body, you have transcended the body.

Stay in this realm of pure Being for as long as feels comfortable; then become aware again of the physical body, your breathing and physical senses, and open your eyes. Look at your surroundings for a few minutes in a meditative way — that is, without labeling them mentally — and continue to feel the inner body as you do so.

$$\int$$

Having access to that formless realm is truly liberating. It frees you from bondage to form and identification with form. It is life in its undifferentiated state prior to its fragmentation into multiplicity. We may call it the Unmanifested, the invisible Source of all things, the Being within all beings. It is a realm of deep stillness and peace, but also of joy and intense aliveness. Whenever you are present, you become "transparent" to some extent to the light, the pure consciousness that emanates from this Source. You also realize that the light is not separate from who you are but constitutes your very essence.

THE SOURCE OF CHI

Is the Unmanifested what in the East is called chi, a kind of universal life energy?

No, it isn't. The Unmanifested is the *source* of chi. Chi is the inner energy field of your body. It is the bridge between the outer you and the Source. It lies halfway between the manifested, the world of form, and the Unmanifested. Chi can be likened to a river or an energy stream. If you take the focus of your consciousness deeply into the inner body, you are tracing the course of this river back to its Source. Chi is movement; the Unmanifested is stillness. When you reach a point of absolute stillness, which is nevertheless vibrant with life, you have gone beyond the inner body and beyond chi to the Source itself: the Unmanifested. Chi is the link between the Unmanifested and the physical universe.

So if you take your attention deeply into the inner body, you may reach this point, this singularity, where the world dissolves into the Unmanifested and the Unmanifested takes on form as the energy stream of chi, which then becomes the world. This is the point of birth and death. When your consciousness is directed outward, mind and world arise. When it is directed inward, it realizes its own Source and returns home into the Unmanifested. Then, when your consciousness comes back to the manifested world, you reassume the form identity that you temporarily relinquished. You have a name, a past, a life situation, a future. But in one essential respect, you are not the same person you were before: You will have glimpsed a reality within yourself that is not "of this world," although it isn't separate from it, just as it isn't separate from you.

Now let your spiritual practice be this: As you go about your life, don't give 100 percent of your attention to the external world and to your mind. Keep some within. I have spoken about this already. Feel the inner body even when engaged in everyday activities, especially when engaged in relationships or when you are relating with nature. Feel the stillness deep inside it. Keep the portal open. It is quite possible to be conscious of the Unmanifested throughout your life. You feel it as a deep sense of peace somewhere in the background, a stillness that never leaves you, no matter what happens out here. You become a bridge between the Unmanifested and the manifested, between God and the world. This is the state of connectedness with the Source that we call enlightenment.

Don't get the impression that the Unmanifested is separate from the manifested. How could it be? It is the life within every form, the inner essence of all that exists. It pervades this world. Let me explain.

DREAMLESS SLEEP

You take a journey into the Unmanifested every night when you enter the phase of deep dreamless sleep. You merge with the Source. You draw from it the vital energy that sustains you for a while when you return to the manifested, the world of separate forms. This energy is much more vital than food: "Man does not live by bread alone." But in dreamless sleep, you don't go into it consciously. Although the bodily functions are still operating, "you" no longer exist in that state. Can you imagine what it would be like to go into dreamless sleep with full consciousness? It is impossible to imagine it, because that state has no content.

The Unmanifested does not liberate you until you enter it consciously. That's why Jesus did not say: the truth will make you free, but rather: "You will know the truth, and the truth will make you free." This is not a conceptual truth. It is the truth of eternal life beyond form, which is known directly or not at all. But don't attempt to stay conscious in dreamless sleep. It is highly unlikely that you will succeed. At most, you may remain conscious during the dream phase, but not beyond that. This is called lucid dreaming, which may be interesting and fascinating, but it is not liberating.

So use your inner body as a portal through which you enter the Unmanifested, and keep that portal open so that you stay connected with the Source at all times. It makes no difference, as far as the inner body is concerned, whether your outer physical body is old or young, frail or strong. The inner body is timeless. If you are not yet able to feel the inner body, use one of the other portals, although ultimately they are all one. Some I have spoken about at length already, but I'll mention them again briefly here.

OTHER PORTALS

The Now can be seen as the main portal. It is an essential aspect of every other portal, including the inner body. You cannot be *in your body* without being intensely present in the Now.

Time and the manifested are as inextricably linked as are the timeless Now and the Unmanifested. When you dissolve psychological time through intense present-moment awareness, you become conscious of the Unmanifested both directly and indirectly. Directly, you feel it as the radiance and power of your conscious presence — no content, just presence. Indirectly, you are aware of the Unmanifested in and through the sensory realm. In other words, you feel the God-essence in every creature, every flower, every stone, and you realize: "All that is, is holy." This is why Jesus, speaking entirely from his essence or Christ identity, says in the Gospel of Thomas: "Split a piece of wood; I am there. Lift up a stone, and you will find me there."

Another portal into the Unmanifested is created through the cessation of thinking. This can start with a very simple thing, such as taking one conscious breath or looking, in a state of intense alertness, at a flower, so that there is no mental commentary running at the same time. There are many ways to create a gap in the incessant stream of thought. This is what meditation is all about. Thought is part of the realm of the manifested. Continuous mind activity keeps you imprisoned in the world of form and becomes an opaque screen that prevents you from becoming conscious of the Unmanifested, conscious of the formless and timeless God-essence in yourself and in all things and all creatures. When you are intensely *present*, you don't need to be concerned about the cessation of thinking, of course, because the mind then stops automatically. That's why I said the Now is an essential aspect of every other portal.

Surrender — the letting go of mental-emotional resistance to what *is* — also becomes a portal into the Unmanifested. The reason for this is simple: inner resistance cuts you off from other people, from yourself, from the world around you. It strengthens the feeling of separateness on which the ego depends for its survival. The stronger the feeling of separateness, the more you are bound to the manifested, to the world of separate forms. The more you are bound to the world of form, the harder and more impenetrable your form identity becomes. The portal is closed, and you are cut off from the inner dimension, the dimension of depth. In the state of surrender, your form identity softens and becomes somewhat "transparent," as it were, so the Unmanifested can shine through you.

It's up to you to open a portal in your life that gives you conscious access to the Unmanifested. Get in touch with the energy field of the inner body, be intensely present, disidentify from the mind, surrender to what *is*; these are all portals you can use — but you only need to use one.

Surely love must also be one of those portals?

No, it isn't. As soon as one of the portals is open, love is present in you as the "feeling-realization" of oneness. Love isn't a portal; it's what comes *through* the portal into this world. As long as you are completely trapped in your form identity, there can be no love. Your task is not to search for love but to find a portal through which love can enter.

SILENCE

Are there any other portals apart from those you just mentioned?

Yes, there are. The Unmanifested is not separate from the manifested. It pervades this world, but it is so well disguised that almost everybody misses it completely. If you know where to look, you'll find it everywhere. A portal opens up every moment.

Do you hear that dog barking in the distance? Or that car passing by? Listen carefully. Can you feel the presence of the Unmanifested in that? You can't? Look for it in the silence out of which the sounds come and into which they return. Pay more attention to the silence than to the sounds. Paying attention to outer silence creates inner silence: the mind becomes still. A portal is opening up.

Every sound is born out of silence, dies back into silence, and during its life span is surrounded by silence. Silence enables the sound to be. It is an intrinsic but unmanifested part of every sound, every musical note, every song, every word. The Unmanifested is present in this world as silence. This is why it has been said that nothing in this world is so like God as silence. All you have to do is pay attention to it. Even during a conversation, become conscious of the gaps between words, the brief silent intervals between sentences. As you do that, the dimension of stillness grows within you. You cannot pay attention to silence without simultaneously becoming still within. Silence without, stillness within. You have entered the Unmanifested.

SPACE

Just as no sound can exist without silence, nothing can exist without no-thing, without the empty space that enables it to be. Every physical object or body has come out of nothing, is surrounded by nothing, and will eventually return to nothing. Not only that, but even inside every physical body there is far more "nothing" than "something." Physicists tell us that the solidity of matter is an illusion. Even seemingly solid matter, including your physical body, is nearly 100 percent empty space — so vast are the distances between the atoms compared to their size. What is more, even inside every atom there is mostly empty space. What is left is more like a vibrational frequency than particles of solid matter, more like a musical note. Buddhists have known that for over 2,500 years. "Form is emptiness, emptiness is form," states the *Heart Sutra*, one of the best known ancient Buddhist texts. The essence of all things is emptiness.

The Unmanifested is not only present in this world as silence; it also pervades the entire physical universe as space — from within and without. This is just as easy to miss as silence. Everybody pays attention to the things in space, but who pays attention to space itself?

You seem to be implying that "emptiness" or "nothing" is not just nothing, that there is some mysterious quality to it. What is this nothing?

You cannot ask such a question. Your mind is trying to make noth- ing into something. The moment you make it into something, you have missed it. Nothing — space — is the appearance of the Unmanifested as an externalized phenomenon in a sense-perceived world. That's about as much as one can say about it, and even that is a kind of paradox. It cannot become an object of knowledge. You can't do a Ph.D. on "nothing." When scientists study space, they usu- ally make it into something and thereby miss its essence entirely. Not surprisingly, the latest theory is that space isn't empty at all, that it is filled with some substance. Once you have a theory, it's not too hard to find evidence to substantiate it, at least until some other theory comes along.

"Nothing" can only become a portal into the Unmanifested for you if you don't try to grasp or understand it.

Isn't that what we are doing here?

Not at all. I am giving you pointers to show you how you can bring the dimension of the Unmanifested into your life. We are not trying to understand it. There is nothing to understand.

Space has no "existence." "To exist" literally means "to stand out." You cannot understand space because it doesn't stand out. Although in itself it has no existence, it enables everything else to exist. Silence has no existence either, nor does the Unmanifested.

So what happens if you withdraw attention from the objects in space and become aware of space itself? What is the essence of this room? The furniture, pictures, and so on are *in* the room, but they are not the room. The floor, walls, and ceiling define the boundary of the room, but they are not the room either. So what is the essence of the room? Space, of course, empty space. There would be no "room" without it. Since space is "nothing," we can say that what is *not* there is more important than what is there. So become aware of the space that is all around you. Don't think about it. Feel it, as it were. Pay attention to "nothing."

As you do that, a shift in consciousness takes place inside you. Here is why. The inner equivalent to objects in space such as furniture, walls, and so on are your mind objects: thoughts, emotions, and the objects of the senses. And the inner equivalent of space is the consciousness that enables your mind objects to be, just as space allows all things to be. So if you withdraw attention from *things* — objects in space — you automatically withdraw attention from your mind objects as well. In other words: You cannot think *and* be aware of space — or of silence, for that matter. By becoming aware of the empty space around you, you simultaneously become aware of the space of no-mind, of pure consciousness: the Unmanifested. This is how the contemplation of space can become a portal for you.

Space and silence are two aspects of the same thing, the same nothing. They are an externalization of inner space and inner silence, which is stillness: the infinitely creative womb of all existence. Most humans are completely unconscious of this dimension. There is no inner space, no stillness. They are out of balance. In other words, they know the world, or think they do, but they don't know God. They identify exclusively with their own physical and psychological form, unconscious of essence. And because every form is highly unstable, they live in fear. This fear causes a deep misperception of themselves and of other humans, a distortion in their vision of the world.

If some cosmic convulsion brought about the end of our world, the Unmanifested would remain totally unaffected by this. *A Course in Miracles* expresses this truth poignantly: "Nothing real can be threatened. Nothing unreal exists. Herein lies the peace of God."

If you remain in conscious connection with the Unmanifested, you value, love, and deeply respect the manifested and every life form in it as an expression of the One Life beyond form. You also know that every form is destined to dissolve again and that ultimately nothing out here matters all that much. You have "overcome the world," in the words of Jesus, or, as the Buddha put it, you have "crossed over to the other shore."

THE TRUE NATURE OF SPACE AND TIME

Now consider this: If there were nothing but silence, it wouldn't exist for you; you wouldn't know what it is. Only when sound appears does silence come into being. Similarly, if there were only space without any objects in space, it wouldn't exist for you. Imagine yourself as a point of consciousness floating in the vastness of space — no stars, no galaxies, just emptiness. Suddenly, space wouldn't be vast anymore; it would not be there at all. There would be no speed, no movement from here to there. At least two points of reference are needed for distance and space to come into being. Space comes into being the moment the One becomes two, and as "two" become the "ten thousand things," as Lao Tse calls the manifested world, space becomes more and more vast. So world and space arise simultaneously.

Nothing could *be* without space, yet space is nothing. Before the universe came into being, before the "big bang" if you like, there wasn't a vast empty space waiting to be filled. There was no space, as there was no thing. There was only the Unmanifested — the One. When the One became "the ten thousand things," suddenly space seemed to be there and enabled the many to be. Where did it come from? Was it created by God to accommodate the universe? Of course not. Space is no-thing, so it was never created.

Go out on a clear night and look up at the sky. The thousands of stars you can see with the naked eye are no more than an infinitesimal fraction of what is there. One thousand million galaxies can already be detected with the most powerful telescopes, each galaxy an "island universe" containing thousands of millions of stars. Yet what is even more awe-inspiring is the infinity of space itself, the depth and stillness that allows all of that magnificence to be. Nothing could be more awe-inspiring and majestic than the inconceivable vastness and stillness of space, and yet what is it? Emptiness, vast emptiness.

What appears to us as space in our universe perceived through the mind and the senses is the Unmanifested itself, externalized. It is the "body" of God. And the greatest miracle is this: That stillness and vastness that enables the universe to *be*, is not just out there in space — it is also within you. When you are utterly and totally *present*, you encounter it as the still inner space of no-mind. Within you, it is vast in depth, not in extension. Spacial extension is ultimately a mis-perception of infinite depth — an attribute of the one transcendental reality.

According to Einstein, space and time are not separate. I don't really understand it, but I think he is saying that time is the fourth dimen-sion of space. He calls it the "space-time continuum."

Yes. What you perceive externally as space and time are ultimately illusory, but they contain a core of truth. They are the two essential attributes of God, infinity and eternity, perceived as if they had an external existence outside you. Within you, both space and time have an inner equivalent that reveals their true nature, as well as your own. Whereas space is the still, infinitely deep realm of no-mind, the inner equivalent of time is presence, awareness of the eternal Now. Remember that there is no distinction between them. When space and time are realized within as the Unmanifested — no-mind and presence — external space and time continue to exist for you, but they become much less important. The world, too, continues to exist for you, but it will not bind you anymore.

Hence, the ultimate purpose of the world lies not within the world but in transcendence of the world. Just as you would not be conscious of space if there were no objects in space, the world is needed for the Unmanifested to be realized. You may have heard the Buddhist saying: "If there were no illusion, there would be no enlightenment." It is through the world and ultimately through *you* that the Unmanifested knows itself. You are here to enable the divine purpose of the universe to unfold. *That is how important you are!*

CONSCIOUS DEATH

Apart from dreamless sleep, which I mentioned already, there is one other involuntary portal. It opens up briefly at the time of physical death. Even if you have missed all the other opportunities for spiritual realization during your lifetime, one last portal will open up for you immediately after the body has died.

There are countless accounts by people who had a visual impression of this portal as radiant light and then returned from what is commonly known as a near-death experience. Many of them also spoke of a sense of blissful serenity and deep peace. In the *Tibetan Book of the Dead*, it is described as "the luminous splendor of the colorless light of Emptiness," which it says is "your own true self." This portal opens up only very briefly, and unless you have already encountered the dimension of the Unmanifested in your lifetime, you will likely miss it. Most people carry too much residual resistance, too much fear, too much attachment to sensory experience, too much identification with the manifested world. So they see the portal, turn away in fear, and then lose consciousness. Most of what happens after that is involuntary and automatic. Eventually, there will be another round of birth and death. Their presence wasn't strong enough yet for conscious immortality.

So going through this portal does not mean annihilation?

As with all the other portals, your radiant true nature remains, but not the personality. In any case, whatever is real or of true value in your personality is your true nature shining through. This is never lost. Nothing that is of value, nothing that is *real*, is ever lost.

Approaching death and death itself, the dissolution of the physical form, is always a great opportunity for spiritual realization. This opportunity is tragically missed most of the time, since we live in a culture that is almost totally ignorant of death, as it is almost totally ignorant of anything that truly matters.

Every portal is a portal of death, the death of the false self. When you go through it, you cease to derive your identity from your psychological, mind-made form. You then realize that death is an illusion, just as your identification with form was an illusion. The end of illusion — that's all that death is. It is painful only as long as you cling to illusion.

CHAPTER EIGHT

ENLIGHTENED RELATIONSHIPS

ENTER THE NOW FROM WHEREVER YOU ARE

I always thought that true enlightenment is not possible except through love in a relationship between a man and a woman. Isn't this what makes us whole again? How can one's life be fulfilled until that happens?

Is that true in your experience? Has this happened to you?

Not yet, but how could it be otherwise? I know that it will happen.

In other words, you are waiting for an event *in time* to save you. Is this not the core error that we have been talking about? Salvation is not elsewhere in place or time. It is here and now.

What does that statement mean, "salvation is here and now"? I don't understand it. I don't even know what salvation means.

Most people pursue physical pleasures or various forms of psychological gratification because they believe that those things will make them happy or free them from a feeling of fear or lack. Happiness may be perceived as a heightened sense of aliveness attained through physical pleasure, or a more secure and more complete sense of self attained through some form of psychological gratification. This is the search for salvation from a state of unsatisfactoriness or insufficiency. Invariably, any satisfaction that they obtain is short-lived, so the condition of satisfaction or fulfillment is usually projected once again onto an imaginary point away from the here and now. "When I obtain *this* or am free of *that* — then I will be okay." This is the unconscious mind-set that creates the illusion of salvation in the future.

True salvation is fulfillment, peace, life in all its fullness. It is to be who you are, to feel within you the good that has no opposite, the joy of Being that depends on nothing outside itself. It is felt not as a passing experience but as an abiding presence. In theistic language, it is to "know God" — not as something outside you but as your own innermost essence. True salvation is to know yourself as an inseparable part of the timeless and formless One Life from which all that exists derives its being.

True salvation is a state of freedom — from fear, from suffering, from a perceived state of lack and insufficiency and therefore from all wanting, needing, grasping, and clinging. It is freedom from compulsive thinking, from negativity, and above all from past and future as a psychological need. Your mind is telling you that you cannot get there from here. Something needs to happen, or you need to become this or that before you can be free and fulfilled. It is saying, in fact, that you need time — that you need to find, sort out, do, achieve, acquire, become, or understand something before you can be free or complete. You see time as the means to salvation, whereas in truth it is the greatest obstacle to salvation. You think that you can't get there from where and who you are at this moment because you are not yet complete or good enough, but the truth is that here and now is the only point from where you *can* get there. You "get" there by realizing that you *are* there already. You find God the moment you realize that you don't need to seek God. So there is no *only* way to salvation: Any condition can be used, but no particular condition is needed. However, there is only one point of access: the Now. There can be no salvation away from this moment. You are lonely and without a partner? Enter the Now from there. You are in a relationship? Enter the Now from there.

There is nothing you can ever do or attain that will get you closer to salvation than it is at this moment. This may be hard to grasp for a mind accustomed to thinking that everything worthwhile is in the future. Nor can anything that you ever did or that was done to you in the past prevent you from saying yes to what *is* and taking your attention deeply into the Now. You cannot do this in the future. You do it now or not at all.

∫

LOVE/HATE RELATIONSHIPS

Unless and until you access the consciousness frequency of presence, all relationships, and particularly intimate relationships, are deeply flawed and ultimately dysfunctional. They may seem perfect for a while, such as when you are "in love," but invariably that apparent perfection gets disrupted as arguments, conflicts, dissatisfaction, and emotional or even physical violence occur with increasing frequency. It seems that most "love relationships" become love/hate relationships before long. Love can then turn into savage attack, feelings of hostility, or complete withdrawal of affection at the flick of a switch. This is considered normal. The relationship then oscillates for a while, a few months or a few years, between the polarities of "love" and hate, and it gives you as much pleasure as it gives you pain. It is not uncommon for couples to become addicted to those cycles. Their drama makes them feel alive. When a balance between the positive/negative polarities is lost and the negative, destructive cycles occur with increasing frequency and intensity, which tends to happen sooner or later, then it will not be long before the relationship finally collapses.

It may appear that if you could only eliminate the negative or destructive cycles, then all would be well and the relationship would flower beautifully — but alas, this is not possible. The polarities are mutually interdependent. You cannot have one without the other. The positive already contains within itself the as yet unmanifested negative. Both are in fact different aspects of the same dysfunction. I am speaking here of what is commonly called romantic relationships — not of true love, which has no opposite because it arises from beyond the mind. Love as a continuous state is as yet very rare — as rare as conscious human beings. Brief and elusive glimpses of love, however, are possible whenever there is a gap in the stream of mind.

The negative side of a relationship is, of course, more easily recognizable as dysfunctional than the positive one. And it is also easier to recognize the source of negativity in your partner than to see it in yourself. It can manifest in many forms: possessiveness, jealousy, control, withdrawal and unspoken resentment, the need to be right, insensitivity and self-absorption, emotional demands and manipulation, the urge to argue, criticize, judge, blame, or attack, anger, unconscious revenge for past pain inflicted by a parent, rage and physical violence.

On the positive side, you are "in love" with your partner. This is at first a deeply satisfying state. You feel intensely alive. Your existence has suddenly become meaningful because someone needs you, wants you, and makes you feel special, and you do the same for him or her. When you are together, you feel whole. The feeling can become so intense that the rest of the world fades into insignificance.

However, you may also have noticed that there is a neediness and a clinging quality to that intensity. You become addicted to the other person. He or she acts on you like a drug. You are on a high when the drug is available, but even the possibility or the thought that he or she might no longer be there for you can lead to jealousy, possessiveness, attempts at manipulation through emotional blackmail, blaming and accusing — fear of loss. If the other person does leave you, this can give rise to the most intense hostility or the most profound grief and despair. In an instant, loving tenderness can turn into a savage attack or dreadful grief. Where is the love now? Can love change into its opposite in an instant? Was it love in the first place, or just an addictive grasping and clinging?

ADDICTION AND THE SEARCH FOR WHOLENESS

Why should we become addicted to another person?

The reason why the romantic love relationship is such an intense and universally sought-after experience is that it seems to offer liberation from a deep-seated state of fear, need, lack, and incompleteness that is part of the human condition in its unredeemed and unenlightened state. There is a physical as well as a psychological dimension to this state.

On the physical level, you are obviously not whole, nor will you ever be: You are either a man or a woman, which is to say, one-half of the whole. On this level, the longing for wholeness — the return to oneness — manifests as male-female attraction, man's need for a woman, woman's need for a man. It is an almost irresistible urge for union with the opposite energy polarity. The root of this physical urge is a spiritual one: the longing for an end to duality, a return to the state of wholeness. Sexual union is the closest you can get to this state on the physical level. This is why it is the most deeply satisfying experience the physical realm can offer. But sexual union is no more than a fleeting glimpse of wholeness, an instant of bliss. As long as it is unconsciously sought as a means of salvation, you are seeking the end of duality on the level of form, where it cannot be found. You are given a tantalizing glimpse of heaven, but you are not allowed to dwell there, and find yourself again in a separate body.

On the psychological level, the sense of lack and incompleteness is, if anything, even greater than on the physical level. As long as you are identified with the mind, you have an externally derived sense of self. That is to say, you get your sense of who you are from things that ultimately have nothing to do with who you are: your social role, possessions, external appearance, successes and failures, belief systems, and so on. This false, mind-made self, the ego, feels vulnerable, insecure, and is always seeking new things to identify with to give it a feeling that it exists. But nothing is ever enough to give it lasting fulfillment. Its fear remains; its sense of lack and neediness remains.

But then that special relationship comes along. It seems to be the answer to all the ego's problems and to meet all its needs. At least this is how it appears at first. All the other things that you derived your sense of self from before, now become relatively insignificant. You now have a single focal point that replaces them all, gives meaning to your life, and through which you define your identity: the person you are "in love" with. You are no longer a disconnected fragment in an uncaring universe, or so it seems. Your world now has a center: the loved one. The fact that the center is outside you and that, therefore, you still have an externally derived sense of self does not seem to matter at first. What matters is that the underlying feelings of incompleteness, of fear, lack and unfulfillment so characteristic of the egoic state are no longer there — or are they? Have they dissolved, or do they continue to exist underneath the happy surface reality?

If in your relationships you experience both "love" and the opposite of love — attack, emotional violence, and so on — then it is likely that you are confusing ego attachment and addictive clinging with love. You cannot love your partner one moment and attack him or her the next. True love has no opposite. If your "love" has an opposite, then it is not love but a strong ego-need for a more complete and deeper sense of self, a need that the other person temporarily meets. It is the ego's substitute for salvation, and for a short time it almost does feel like salvation.

But there comes a point when your partner behaves in ways that fail to meet your needs, or rather those of your ego. The feelings of fear, pain, and lack that are an intrinsic part of egoic consciousness but had been covered up by the "love relationship" now resurface. Just as with every other addiction, you are on a high when the drug is available, but invariably there comes a time when the drug no longer works for you. When those painful feelings reappear, you feel them even more strongly than before, and what is more, you now perceive your partner as the *cause* of those feelings. This means that you project them outward and attack the other with all the savage violence that is part of your pain. This attack may awaken the partner's own pain, and he or she may counter your attack. At this point, the ego is still unconsciously hoping that its attack or its attempts at manipulation will be sufficient punishment to induce your partner to change their behavior, so that it can use them again as a cover-up for your pain.

Every addiction arises from an unconscious refusal to face and move through your own pain. Every addiction starts with pain and ends with pain. Whatever the substance you are addicted to — alcohol, food, legal or illegal drugs, or a person — you are using something or somebody to cover up your pain. That is why, after the initial euphoria has passed, there is so much unhappiness, so much pain in intimate relationships. They do not cause pain and unhappiness. They *bring out* the pain and unhappiness that is already in you. Every addiction does that. Every addiction reaches a point where it does not work for you anymore, and then you feel the pain more intensely than ever.

This is one reason why most people are always trying to escape from the present moment and are seeking some kind of salvation in the future. The first thing that they might encounter if they focused their attention on the Now is their own pain, and this is what they fear. If they only knew how easy it is to access in the Now the power of presence that dissolves the past and its pain, the reality that dissolves the illusion. If they only knew how close they are to their own reality, how close to God.

Avoidance of relationships in an attempt to avoid pain is not the answer either. The pain is there anyway. Three failed relationships in as many years are more likely to force you into awakening than three years on a desert island or shut away in your room. But if you could bring intense presence into your aloneness, that would work for you too.

THE POWER OF NOW

FROM ADDICTIVE TO ENLIGHTENED RELATIONSHIPS

Can we change an addictive relationship into a true one?

Yes. Being present and intensifying your presence by taking your attention ever more deeply into the Now: Whether you are living alone or with a partner, this remains the key. For love to flourish, the light of your presence needs to be strong enough so that you no longer get taken over by the thinker or the pain-body and mistake them for who you are. To know yourself as the Being underneath the thinker, the stillness underneath the mental noise, the love and joy underneath the pain, is freedom, salvation, enlightenment. To disidentify from the pain-body is to bring presence into the pain and thus transmute it. To disidentify from thinking is to be the silent watcher of your thoughts and behavior, especially the repetitive patterns of your mind and the roles played by the ego.

If you stop investing it with "selfness," the mind loses its compulsive quality, which basically is the compulsion to judge, and so to resist what *is*, which creates conflict, drama, and new pain. In fact, the moment that judgment stops through acceptance of what *is*, you are free of the mind. You have made room for love, for joy, for peace. First you stop judging yourself; then you stop judging your partner. The greatest catalyst for change in a relationship is complete acceptance of your partner as he or she is, without needing to judge or change them in any way. That immediately takes you beyond ego. All mind games and all addictive clinging are then over. There are no victims and no perpetrators anymore, no accuser and accused. This is also the end of all codependency, of being drawn into somebody else's unconscious pattern and thereby enabling it to continue. You will then either separate — in love — or move ever more deeply into the Now together — into Being. Can it be that simple? Yes, it is that simple.

Love is a state of Being. Your love is not outside; it is deep within you. You can never lose it, and it cannot leave you. It is not dependent on some other body, some external form. In the stillness of your presence, you can feel your own formless and timeless reality as the unmanifested life that animates your physical form. You can then feel the same life deep within every other human and every other creature. You look beyond the veil of form and separation. This is the realization of oneness. This is love.

What is God? The eternal One Life underneath all the forms of life. What is love? To feel the presence of that One Life deep within yourself and within all creatures. To be it. Therefore, all love is the love of God.

Love is not selective, just as the light of the sun is not selective. It does not make one person special. It is not exclusive. Exclusivity is not the love of God but the "love" of ego. However, the intensity with which true love is felt can vary. There may be one person who reflects your love back to you more clearly and more intensely than others, and if that person feels the same toward you, it can be said that you are in a love relationship with him or her. The bond that connects you with that person is the same bond that connects you with the person sitting next to you on a bus, or with a bird, a tree, a flower. Only the degree of intensity with which it is felt differs.

Even in an otherwise addictive relationship, there may be moments when something more real shines through, something beyond your mutual addictive needs. These are moments when both your and your partner's mind briefly subside and the pain-body is temporarily in a dormant state. This may sometimes happen during physical intimacy, or when you are both witnessing the miracle of childbirth, or in the presence of death, or when one of you is seriously ill — anything that renders the mind powerless. When this happens, your Being, which is usually buried underneath the mind, becomes revealed, and it is this that makes true communication possible.

True communication is communion — the realization of oneness, which is love. Usually, this is quickly lost again, unless you are able to stay present enough to keep out the mind and its old patterns. As soon as the mind and mind identification return, you are no longer yourself but a mental image of yourself, and you start playing games and roles again to get your ego needs met. You are a human mind again, pretending to be a human being, interacting with another mind, playing a drama called "love."

Although brief glimpses are possible, love cannot flourish unless you are permanently free of mind identification and your presence is intense enough to have dissolved the pain-body — or you can at least remain present as the watcher. The pain-body cannot then take you over and so become destructive of love.

RELATIONSHIPS AS SPIRITUAL PRACTICE

As the egoic mode of consciousness and all the social, political, and economic structures that it created enter the final stage of collapse, the relationships between men and women reflect the deep state of crisis in which humanity now finds itself. As humans have become increasingly identified with their mind, most relationships are not rooted in Being and so turn into a source of pain and become dominated by problems and conflict.

Millions are now living alone or as single parents, unable to establish an intimate relationship or unwilling to repeat the insane drama of past relationships. Others go from one relationship to another, from one pleasure-and-pain cycle to another, in search of the elusive goal of fulfillment through union with the opposite energy polarity. Still others compromise and continue to be together in a dysfunctional relationship in which negativity prevails, for the sake of the children or security, through force of habit, fear of being alone, or some other mutually "beneficial" arrangement, or even through the unconscious addiction to the excitement of emotional drama and pain.

However, every crisis represents not only danger but also opportunity. If relationships energize and magnify egoic mind patterns and activate the pain-body, as they do at this time, why not accept this fact rather than try to escape from it? Why not cooperate with it instead of avoiding relationships or continuing to pursue the phantom of an ideal partner as an answer to your problems or a means of feeling fulfilled? The opportunity that is concealed within every crisis does not manifest until all the facts of any given situation are acknowledged and fully accepted. As long as you deny them, as long as you try to escape from them or wish that things were different, the window of opportunity does not open up, and you remain trapped inside that situation, which will remain the same or deteriorate further.

With the acknowledgment and acceptance of the facts also comes a degree of freedom from them. For example, when you *know* there is disharmony and you hold that "knowing," through your knowing a new factor has come in, and the disharmony cannot remain unchanged. When you *know* you are not at peace, your knowing creates a still space that surrounds your nonpeace in a loving and tender embrace and then transmutes your nonpeace into peace. As far as inner transformation is concerned, there is nothing you can *do* about it. You cannot transform yourself, and you certainly cannot transform your partner or anybody else. All you *can* do is create a space for transformation to happen, for grace and love to enter.

So whenever your relationship is not working, whenever it brings out the "madness" in you and in your partner, be glad. What was unconscious is being brought up to the light. It is an opportunity for salvation. Every moment, hold the knowing of that moment, particularly of your inner state. If there is anger, *know* that there is anger. If there is jealousy, defensiveness, the urge to argue, the need to be right, an inner child demanding love and attention, or emotional pain of any kind — whatever it is, *know* the reality of that moment and hold the knowing. The relationship then becomes your *sadhana*, your spiritual practice. If you observe unconscious behavior in your partner, hold it in the loving embrace of your knowing so that you won't react. Unconsciousness and knowing cannot coexist for long — even if the knowing is only in the other person and not in the one who is acting out the unconsciousness. The energy form that lies behind hostility and attack finds the presence of love absolutely intolerable. If you react at all to your partner's unconsciousness, you become unconscious yourself. But if you then remember to *know* your reaction, nothing is lost.

Humanity is under great pressure to evolve because it is our only chance of survival as a race. This will affect every aspect of your life and close relationships in particular. Never before have relationships been as problematic and conflict ridden as they are now. As you may have noticed, they are not here to make you happy or fulfilled. If you continue to pursue the goal of salvation through a relationship, you will be disillusioned again and again. But if you accept that the relationship is here to make you *conscious* instead of happy, then the relationship *will* offer you salvation, and you will be aligning yourself with the higher consciousness that wants to be born into this world. For those who hold on to the old patterns, there will be increasing pain, violence, confusion, and madness.

I suppose that it takes two to make a relationship into a spiritual practice, as you suggest. For example, my partner is still acting out his old patterns of jealousy and control. I have pointed this out many times, but he is unable to see it.

How many people does it take to make your life into a spiritual practice? Never mind if your partner will not cooperate. Sanity — consciousness — can only come into this world through you. You do not need to wait for the world to become sane, or for somebody else to become conscious, before you can be enlightened. You may wait forever. Do not accuse each other of being unconscious. The moment you start to argue, you have identified with a mental position and are now defending not only that position but also your sense of self. The ego is in charge. You have become unconscious. At times, it may be appropriate to point out certain aspects of your partner's behavior. If you are very alert, very present, you can do so without ego involvement — without blaming, accusing, or making the other wrong.

When your partner behaves unconsciously, relinquish all judgment. Judgment is either to confuse someone's unconscious behavior with who they are or to project your own unconsciousness onto another person and mistake *that* for who they are. To relinquish judgment does not mean that you do not recognize dysfunction and unconsciousness when you see it. It means "being the knowing" rather than "being the reaction" and the judge. You will then either be totally free of reaction or you may react and still be the knowing, the space in which the reaction is watched and allowed to be. Instead of fighting the darkness, you bring in the light. Instead of reacting to delusion, you see the delusion yet at the same time look through it. Being the knowing creates a clear space of loving presence that allows all things and all people to be as they are. No greater catalyst for transformation exists. If you practice this, your partner cannot stay with you *and* remain unconscious.

If you both agree that the relationship will be your spiritual practice, so much the better. You can then express your thoughts and feelings to each other as soon as they occur, or as soon as a reaction comes up, so that you do not create a time gap in which an unexpressed or unacknowledged emotion or grievance can fester and grow. Learn to give expression to what you feel without blaming. Learn to listen to your partner in an open, nondefensive way. Give your partner space for expressing himself or herself. Be present. Accusing, defending, attacking — all those patterns that are designed to strengthen or protect the ego or to get its needs met will then become redundant. Giving space to others — and to yourself — is vital. Love cannot flourish without it. When you have removed the two factors that are destructive of relationships: When the pain-body has been transmuted and you are no longer identified with mind and mental positions, and if your partner has done the same, you will experience the bliss of the flowering of relationship. Instead of mirroring to each other your pain and your unconsciousness, instead of satisfying your mutual addictive ego needs, you will reflect back to each other the love that you feel deep within, the love that comes with the realization of your oneness with all that is. This is the love that has no opposite.

If your partner is still identified with the mind and the pain-body while you are already free, this will represent a major challenge — not to you but to your partner. It is not easy to live with an enlightened person, or rather it is *so* easy that the ego finds it extremely threatening. Remember that the ego needs problems, conflict, and "enemies" to strengthen the sense of separateness on which its identity depends. The unenlightened partner's mind will be deeply frustrated because its fixed positions are not resisted, which means they will become shaky and weak, and there is even the "danger" that they may collapse altogether, resulting in loss of self. The pain-body is demanding feedback and not getting it. The need for argument, drama, and conflict is not being met. But beware: Some people who are unresponsive, withdrawn, insensitive, or cut off from their feelings may think and try to convince others that they are enlightened, or at least that there is "nothing wrong" with them and everything wrong with their partner. Men tend to do that more than women. They may see their female partners as irrational or emotional. But if you can feel your emotions, you are not far from the radiant inner body just underneath. If you are mainly in your head, the distance is much greater, and you need to bring consciousness into the emotional body before you can reach the inner body.

If there isn't an emanation of love and joy, complete presence and openness toward all beings, then it is not enlightenment. Another indicator is how a person behaves in difficult or challenging situations or when things "go wrong." If your "enlightenment" is egoic self-delusion, then life will soon give you a challenge that will bring out your unconsciousness in whatever form — as fear, anger, defensiveness, judgment, depression, and so on. If you are in a relationship, many of your challenges will come through your partner. For example, a woman may be challenged by an unresponsive male partner who lives almost entirely in his head. She will be challenged by his inability to *hear* her, to give her attention and space to be, which is due to his lack of presence. The absence of love in the relationship, which is usually more keenly felt by a woman than a man, will trigger the woman's pain-body, and through it she will attack her partner — blame, criticize, make wrong, and so on. This in turn now becomes *his* challenge. To defend himself against her pain-body's attack, which he sees as totally unwarranted, he will become even more deeply entrenched in his mental positions as he justifies, defends himself or counterattacks. Eventually, this may activate his own pain-body. When both partners have thus been taken over, a level of deep unconsciousness has been reached, of emotional violence, savage attack and counterattack. It will not subside until both pain-bodies have replenished themselves and then enter the dormant stage. Until the next time.

This is only one of an endless number of possible scenarios. Many volumes have been written, and many more could be written, about the ways in which unconsciousness is brought out in male-female relationships. But, as I said earlier, once you understand the root of the dysfunction, you do not need to explore its countless manifestations.

Let's briefly look again at the scenario I have just described. Every challenge that it contains is actually a disguised opportunity for salvation. At every stage of the unfolding dysfunctional process, freedom from unconsciousness is possible. For example, the woman's hostility could become a signal for the man to come out of his mind-identified state, awaken into the Now, become present — instead of becoming even more identified with his mind, even more unconscious. Instead of "being" the pain-body, the woman could be the knowing that watches the emotional pain in herself, thus accessing the power of the Now and initiating the transmutation of the pain. This would remove the compulsive and automatic outward projection of it. She could then express her feelings to her partner. There is no guarantee, of course, that he will listen, but it gives him a good chance to become present and certainly breaks the insane cycle of the involuntary acting out of old mind patterns. If the woman misses that opportunity, the man could watch his own mental-emotional reaction to her pain, his own defensiveness, rather than *being* the reaction. He could then watch his own pain-body being triggered and thus bring consciousness into his emotions. In this way, a clear and still space of pure awareness would come into being — the knowing, the silent witness, the watcher. This awareness does not deny the pain and yet is beyond it. It allows the pain to be and yet transmutes it at the same time. It accepts everything and transforms everything. A door would have opened up for her through which she could easily join him in that space.

If you are consistently or at least predominantly present in your relationship, this will be the greatest challenge for your partner. They will not be able to tolerate your presence for very long and stay unconscious. If they are ready, they will walk through the door that you opened for them and join you in that state. If they are not, you will separate like oil and water. The light is too painful for someone who wants to remain in darkness.

WHY WOMEN ARE CLOSER TO ENLIGHTENMENT

Are the obstacles to enlightenment the same for a man as for a woman?

Yes, but the emphasis is different. Generally speaking, it is easier for a woman to feel and be in her body, so she is naturally closer to Being and potentially closer to enlightenment than a man. This is why many ancient cultures instinctively chose female figures or analogies to represent or describe the formless and transcendental reality. It was often seen as a womb that gives birth to everything in creation and sustains and nourishes it during its life as form. In the *Tao Te Ching*, one of the most ancient and profound books ever written, the *Tao*, which could be translated as *Being*, is described as "infinite, eternally present, the mother of the universe." Naturally, women are closer to it than men since they virtually "embody" the Unmanifested. What is more, all creatures and all things must eventually return to the Source. "All things vanish into the Tao. It alone endures." Since the Source is seen as female, this is represented as the light and dark sides of the archetypal feminine in psychology and mythology. The Goddess or Divine Mother has two aspects: She gives life, and she takes life.

When the mind took over and humans lost touch with the reality of their divine essence, they started to think of God as a male figure. Society became male dominated, and the female was made subordinate to the male.

I am not suggesting a return to earlier female representations of the divine. Some people now use the term *Goddess* instead of *God*. They are redressing a balance between male and female that was lost a long time ago, and that is good. But it is still a representation and a concept, perhaps temporarily useful, just as a map or a signpost is temporarily useful, but more a hindrance than a help when you are ready to realize the reality beyond all concepts and images. What does remain true, however, is that the energy frequency of the mind appears to be essentially male. The mind resists, fights for control, uses, manipulates, attacks, tries to grasp and possess, and so on. This is why the traditional God is a patriarchal, controlling authority figure, an often angry man who you should live in fear of, as the Old Testament suggests. This God is a projection of the human mind.

To go beyond the mind and reconnect with the deeper reality of Being, very different qualities are needed: surrender, nonjudgment, an openness that allows life to be instead of resisting it, the capacity to hold all things in the loving embrace of your knowing. All these qualities are much more closely related to the female principle. Whereas mind-energy is hard and rigid, Being-energy is soft and yielding and yet infinitely more powerful than mind. The mind runs our civilization, whereas Being is in charge of all life on our planet and beyond. Being is the very Intelligence whose visible manifestation is the physical universe. Although women are potentially closer to it, men can also access it within themselves.

At this time, the vast majority of men as well as women are still in the grip of the mind: identified with the thinker and the pain-body. This, of course, is what prevents enlightenment and the flowering of love. As a general rule, the major obstacle for men tends to be the thinking mind, and the major obstacle for women the pain-body, although in certain individual cases the opposite may be true, and in others the two factors may be equal.

DISSOLVING THE COLLECTIVE FEMALE PAIN-BODY

Why is the pain-body more of an obstacle for women?

The pain-body usually has a collective as well as a personal aspect. The personal aspect is the accumulated residue of emotional pain suffered in one's own past. The collective one is the pain accumulated in the collective human psyche over thousands of years through disease, torture, war, murder, cruelty, madness, and so on. Everyone's personal pain-body also partakes of this collective pain-body. There are different strands in the collective pain-body. For example, certain races or countries in which extreme forms of strife and violence occur have a heavier collective pain-body than others. Anyone with a strong pain-body and not enough consciousness to disidentify from it will not only continuously or periodically be forced to relive their emotional pain but may also easily become either the perpetrator or the victim of violence, depending on whether their pain-body is predominantly active or passive. On the other hand, they may also be potentially closer to enlightenment. This potential isn't necessarily realized, of course, but if you are trapped in a nightmare you will probably be more strongly motivated to awaken than someone who is just caught in the ups and downs of an ordinary dream.

Apart from her personal pain-body, every woman has her share in what could be described as the collective female pain-body — unless she is fully conscious. This consists of accumulated pain suffered by women partly through male subjugation of the female, through slavery, exploitation, rape, childbirth, child loss, and so on, over thousands of years. The emotional or physical pain that for many women precedes and coincides with the menstrual flow is the pain-body in its collective aspect that awakens from its dormancy at that time, although it can be triggered at other times too. It restricts the free flow of life energy through the body, of which menstruation is a physical expression. Let's dwell on this for a moment and see how it can become an opportunity for enlightenment.

Often a woman is "taken over" by the pain-body at that time. It has an extremely powerful energetic charge that can easily pull you into unconscious identification with it. You are then actively possessed by an energy field that occupies your inner space and pretends to be you — but, of course, is not you at all. It speaks through you, acts through you, thinks through you. It will create negative situations in your life so that it can feed on the energy. It wants more pain, in whatever form. I have described this process already. It can be vicious and destructive. It is pure pain, past pain — and it is not you.

The number of women who are now approaching the fully conscious state already exceeds that of men and will be growing even faster in the years to come. Men may catch up with them in the end, but for some considerable time there will be a gap between the consciousness of men and that of women. Women are regaining the function that is their birthright and, therefore, comes to them more naturally than it does to men: to be a bridge between the manifested world and the Unmanifested, between physicality and spirit. Your main task as a woman now is to transmute the pain-body so that it no longer comes between you and your true self, the essence of who you are. Of course, you also have to deal with the other obstacle to enlightenment, which is the thinking mind, but the intense presence you generate when dealing with the pain-body will also free you from identification with the mind.

The first thing to remember is this: As long as you make an identity for yourself out of the pain, you cannot become free of it. As long as part of your sense of self is invested in your emotional pain, you will unconsciously resist or sabotage every attempt that you make to heal that pain. Why? Quite simply because you want to keep yourself intact, and the pain has become an essential part of you. This is an unconscious process, and the only way to overcome it is to make it conscious.

To suddenly see that you are or have been attached to your pain can be quite a shocking realization. The moment you realize this, you have broken the attachment. The pain-body is an energy field, almost like an entity, that has become temporarily lodged in your inner space. It is life energy that has become trapped, energy that is no longer flowing. Of course, the pain-body is there because of certain things that happened in the past. It *is* the living past in you, and if you identify with it, you identify with the past. A victim identity is the belief that the past is more powerful than the present, which is the opposite of the truth. It is the belief that other people and what they did to you are responsible for who you are now, for your emotional pain or your inability to be your true self. The truth is that the only power there is, is contained within this moment: It is the power of your presence. Once you know that, you also realize that *you* are responsible for your inner space now — nobody else is — and that the past cannot prevail against the power of the Now.

So identification prevents you from dealing with the pain-body. Some women who are already conscious enough to have relinquished their victim identity on the personal level are still holding on to a collective victim identity: "what men did to women." They are right — and they are also wrong. They are right inasmuch as the collective female pain-body *is* in large part due to male violence inflicted on women and repression of the female principle throughout the planet over millennia. They are wrong if they derive a sense of self from this fact and thereby keep themselves imprisoned in a collective victim identity. If a woman is still holding on to anger, resentment, or condemnation, she is holding on to her pain-body. This may give her a comforting sense of identity, of solidarity with other women, but it is keeping her in bondage to the past and blocking full access to her essence and true power. If women exclude themselves from men, that fosters a sense of separation and therefore a strengthening of the ego. And the stronger the ego, the more distant you are from your true nature.

So do not use the pain-body to give you an identity. Use it for enlightenment instead. Transmute it into consciousness. One of the best times for this is during menses. I believe that, in the years to come, many women will enter the fully conscious state during that time. Usually, it is a time of unconsciousness for many women, as they are taken over by the collective female pain-body. Once you have reached a certain level of consciousness, however, you can reverse this, so instead of becoming unconscious you become *more* conscious. I have described the basic process already, but let me take you through it again, this time with special reference to the collective female pain-body.

When you know that the menstrual flow is approaching, before you feel the first signs of what is commonly called premenstrual tension, the awakening of the collective female pain-body, become very alert and inhabit your body as fully as possible. When the first sign appears, you need to be alert enough to "catch" it before it takes you over. For example, the first sign may be a sudden strong irritation or a flash of anger, or it may be a purely physical symptom. Whatever it is, catch it before it can take over your thinking or behavior. This simply means putting the spotlight of your attention on it. If it is an emotion, feel the strong energy charge behind it. Know that it is the pain-body. At the same time, be the knowing; that is to say, be aware of your conscious presence and feel its power. Any emotion that you take your presence into will quickly subside and become transmuted. If it is a purely physical symptom, the attention that you give it will prevent it from turning into an emotion or a thought. Then continue to be alert and wait for the next sign of the pain-body. When it appears, catch it again in the same way as before.

Later, when the pain-body has fully awakened from its dormant state, you may experience considerable turbulence in your inner space for a while, perhaps for several days. Whatever form this takes, stay present. Give it your complete attention. Watch the turbulence inside you. Know it is there. Hold the knowing, and be the knowing. Remember: do not let the pain-body use your mind and take over your thinking. Watch it. Feel its energy directly, inside your body. As you know, full attention means full acceptance.

Through sustained attention and thus acceptance, there comes transmutation. The pain-body becomes transformed into radiant consciousness, just as a piece of wood, when placed in or near a fire, itself is transformed into fire. Menstruation will then become not only a joyful and fulfilling expression of your womanhood but also a sacred time of transmutation, when you give birth to a new consciousness. Your true nature then shines forth, both in its female aspect as the Goddess and in its transcendental aspect as the divine Being that you are beyond male and female duality.

If your male partner is conscious enough, he can help you with the practice I have just described by holding the frequency of intense presence particularly at this time. If he stays present whenever you fall back into unconscious identification with the pain-body, which can and will happen at first, you will be able to quickly rejoin him in that state. This means that whenever the pain-body temporarily takes over, whether during menses or at other times, your partner will not mistake it for who you are. Even if the pain-body attacks him, as it probably will, he will not react to it as if it were "you," withdraw, or put up some kind of defense. He will hold the space of intense presence. Nothing else is needed for transformation. At other times, you will be able to do the same for him or help him reclaim consciousness from the mind by drawing his attention into the here and now whenever he becomes identified with his thinking.

In this way, a permanent energy field of a pure and high frequency will arise between you. No illusion, no pain, no conflict, nothing that is not *you*, and nothing that is not love can survive in it. This represents the fulfillment of the divine, transpersonal purpose of your relationship. It becomes a vortex of consciousness that will draw in many others.

$$\int$$

GIVE UP THE RELATIONSHIP WITH YOURSELF

When one is fully conscious, would one still have a need for a relationship? Would a man still feel drawn to a woman? Would a woman still feel incomplete without a man?

Enlightened or not, you are either a man or a woman, so on the level of your form identity you are not complete. You are one-half of the whole. This incompleteness is felt as male-female attraction, the pull toward the opposite energy polarity, no matter how conscious you are. But in that state of inner connectedness, you feel this pull somewhere on the surface or periphery of your life. Anything that happens to you in that state feels somewhat like that. The whole world seems like waves or ripples on the surface of a vast and deep ocean. You are that ocean and, of course, you are also a ripple, but a ripple that has realized its true identity as the ocean, and compared to that vastness and depth, the world of waves and ripples is not all that important.

This does not mean that you don't relate deeply to other people or to your partner. In fact, you can relate deeply *only* if you are conscious of Being. Coming from Being, you are able to focus beyond the veil of form. In Being, male and female are one. Your form may continue to have certain needs, but Being has none. It is already complete and whole. If those needs are met, that is beautiful, but whether or not they are met makes no difference to your deep inner state. So it is perfectly possible for an enlightened person, if the need for the male or female polarity is not met, to feel a sense of lack or incompleteness on the outer level of his or her being, yet at the same time be totally complete, fulfilled, and at peace within.

In the quest for enlightenment, is being gay a help or a hindrance, or does it not make any difference?

As you approach adulthood, uncertainty about your sexuality followed by the realization that you are "different" from others may force you to disidentify from socially conditioned patterns of thought and behavior. This will automatically raise your level of consciousness above that of the unconscious majority, whose members unquestioningly take on board all inherited patterns. In that respect, being gay can be a help. Being an outsider to some extent, someone who does not "fit in" with others or is rejected by them for whatever reason, makes life difficult, but it also places you at an advantage as far as enlightenment is concerned. It takes you out of unconsciousness almost by force.

On the other hand, if you then develop a sense of identity based on your gayness, you have escaped one trap only to fall into another. You will play roles and games dictated by a mental image you have of yourself as gay. You will become unconscious. You will become unreal. Underneath your ego mask, you will become very unhappy. If this happens to you, being gay will have become a hindrance. But you always get another chance, of course. Acute unhappiness can be a great awakener.

Is it not true that you need to have a good relationship with yourself and love yourself before you can have a fulfilling relationship with another person?

If you cannot be at ease with yourself when you are alone, you will seek a relationship to cover up your unease. You can be sure that the unease will then reappear in some other form within the relationship, and you will probably hold your partner responsible for it.

All you really need to do is accept this moment fully. You are then at ease in the here and now and at ease with yourself.

But do you need to have a relationship with yourself at all? Why can't you just *be* yourself? When you have a relationship with yourself, you have split yourself into two: "I" and "myself," subject and object. That mind-created duality is the root cause of all unnecessary complexity, of all problems and conflict in your life. In the state of enlightenment, you *are* yourself — "you" and "yourself" merge into one. You do not judge yourself, you do not feel sorry for yourself, you are not proud of yourself, you do not love yourself, you do not hate yourself, and so on. The split caused by self-reflective consciousness is healed, its curse removed. There is no "self" that you need to protect, defend, or feed anymore. When you are enlightened, there is one relationship that you no longer have: the relationship with yourself. Once you have given that up, all your other relationships will be love relationships.

CHAPTER NINE

BEYOND HAPPINESS AND UNHAPPINESS THERE IS PEACE

THE HIGHER GOOD BEYOND GOOD AND BAD

Is there a difference between happiness and inner peace?

Yes. Happiness depends on conditions being perceived as positive; inner peace does not.

Is it not possible to attract only positive conditions into our life? If our attitude and our thinking are always positive, we would manifest only positive events and situations, wouldn't we?

Do you truly know what is positive and what is negative? Do you have the total picture? There have been many people for whom limitation, failure, loss, illness, or pain in whatever form turned out to be their greatest teacher. It taught them to let go of false self-images and superficial ego-dictated goals and desires. It gave them depth, humility, and compassion. It made them more *real*.

Whenever anything negative happens to you, there is a deep lesson concealed within it, although you may not see it at the time. Even a brief illness or an accident can show you what is real and unreal in your life, what ultimately matters and what doesn't.

Seen from a higher perspective, conditions *are* always positive. To be more precise: they are neither positive nor negative. They are as they are. And when you live in complete acceptance of what *is* — which is the only sane way to live — there is no "good" or "bad" in your life anymore. There is only a higher good — which includes the "bad." Seen from the perspective of the mind, however, there is good-bad, like-dislike, love-hate. Hence, in the Book of Genesis, it is said that Adam and Eve were no longer allowed to dwell in "paradise" when they "ate of the tree of the knowledge of good and evil."

This sounds to me like denial and self-deception. When something dreadful happens to me or someone close to me — accident, illness, pain of some kind or death — I can pretend that it isn't bad, but the fact remains that it is bad, so why deny it?

You are not pretending anything. You are allowing it to be as it is, that's all. This "allowing to be" takes you beyond the mind with its resistance patterns that create the positive-negative polarities. It is an essential aspect of forgiveness. Forgiveness of the present is even more important than forgiveness of the past. If you forgive every moment — allow it to be as it is — then there will be no accumulation of resentment that needs to be forgiven at some later time.

Remember that we are not talking about happiness here. For example, when a loved one has just died, or you feel your own death approaching, you cannot be happy. It is impossible. But you *can* be at peace. There may be sadness and tears, but provided that you have relinquished resistance, underneath the sadness you will feel a deep serenity, a stillness, a sacred presence. This is the emanation of Being, this is inner peace, the good that has no opposite.

What if it is a situation that I can do something about? How can I allow it to be and change it at the same time?

Do what you have to do. In the meantime, accept what *is*. Since mind and resistance are synonymous, acceptance immediately frees you from mind dominance and thus reconnects you with Being. As a result, the usual ego motivations for "doing" — fear, greed, control, defending or feeding the false sense of self — will cease to operate. An intelligence much greater than the mind is now in charge, and so a different quality of consciousness will flow into your doing.

"Accept whatever comes to you woven in the pattern of your destiny, for what could more aptly fit your needs?" This was written 2,000 years ago by Marcus Aurelius, one of those exceedingly rare humans who possessed worldly power as well as wisdom.

It seems that most people need to experience a great deal of suffering before they will relinquish resistance and accept — before they will forgive. As soon as they do, one of the greatest miracles happens: the awakening of Being-consciousness through what appears as evil, the transmutation of suffering into inner peace. The ultimate effect of all the evil and suffering in the world is that it will force humans into realizing who they are beyond name and form. Thus, what we perceive as evil from our limited perspective is actually part of the higher good that has no opposite. This, however, does not become true for you except through forgiveness. Until that happens, evil has not been redeemed and therefore remains evil.

Through forgiveness, which essentially means recognizing the insubstantiality of the past and allowing the present moment to be as it is, the miracle of transformation happens not only within but also without. A silent space of intense presence arises both in you and around you. Whoever or whatever enters that field of consciousness will be affected by it, sometimes visibly and immediately, sometimes at deeper levels with visible changes appearing at a later time. You dissolve discord, heal pain, dispel unconsciousness — without *doing* anything — simply by *being* and holding that frequency of intense presence.

THE END OF YOUR LIFE DRAMA

In that state of acceptance and inner peace, even though you may not call it "bad," can anything still come into your life that would be called "bad" from a perspective of ordinary consciousness?

Most of the so-called bad things that happen in people's lives are due to unconsciousness. They are self-created, or rather ego-created. I sometimes refer to those things as "drama." When you are fully conscious, drama does not come into your life anymore. Let me remind you briefly how the ego operates and how it creates drama.

Ego is the unobserved mind that runs your life when you are not present as the witnessing consciousness, the watcher. The ego perceives itself as a separate fragment in a hostile universe, with no real inner connection to any other being, surrounded by other egos which it either sees as a potential threat or which it will attempt to use for its own ends. The basic ego patterns are designed to combat its own deep-seated fear and sense of lack. They are resistance, control, power, greed, defense, attack. Some of the ego's strategies are extremely clever, yet they never truly solve any of its problems, simply because the ego itself is the problem.

When egos come together, whether in personal relationships or in organizations or institutions, "bad" things happen sooner or later: drama of one kind or another, in the form of conflict, problems, power struggles, emotional or physical violence, and so on. This includes collective evils such as war, genocide, and exploitation — all due to massed unconsciousness. Furthermore, many types of illness are caused by the ego's continuous resistance, which creates restrictions and blockages in the flow of energy through the body. When you reconnect with Being and are no longer run by your mind, you cease to create those things. You do not create or participate in drama anymore.

Whenever two or more egos come together, drama of one kind or another ensues. But even if you live totally alone, you still create your own drama. When you feel sorry for yourself, that's drama. When you feel guilty or anxious, that's drama. When you let the past or future obscure the present, you are creating time, psychological time — the stuff out of which drama is made. Whenever you are not honoring the present moment by allowing it to be, you are creating drama.

Most people are in love with their particular life drama. Their story is their identity. The ego runs their life. They have their whole sense of self invested in it. Even their — usually unsuccessful — search for an answer, a solution, or for healing becomes part of it. What they fear and resist most is the end of their drama. As long as they *are* their mind, what they fear and resist most is their own awakening.

When you live in complete acceptance of what *is*, that is the end of all drama in your life. Nobody can even have an argument with you, no matter how hard he or she tries. You cannot have an argument with a fully conscious person. An argument implies identification with your mind and a mental position, as well as resistance and reaction to the other person's position. The result is that the polar opposites become mutually energized. These are the mechanics of unconsciousness. You can still make your point clearly and firmly, but there will be no reactive force behind it, no defense or attack. So it won't turn into drama. When you are fully conscious, you cease to be in conflict. "No one who is at one with himself can even conceive of conflict," states *A Course in Miracles*. This refers not only to conflict with other people but more fundamentally to conflict within you, which ceases when there is no longer any clash between the demands and expectations of your mind and what *is*.

IMPERMANENCE AND THE CYCLES OF LIFE

However, as long as you are in the physical dimension and linked to the collective human psyche, physical pain — although rare — is still possible. This is not to be confused with suffering, with mental-emotional pain. All suffering is ego-created and is due to resistance. Also, as long as you are in this dimension, you are still subject to its cyclical nature and to the law of impermanence of all things, but you no longer perceive this as "bad" — it just *is*.

Through allowing the "isness" of all things, a deeper dimension underneath the play of opposites reveals itself to you as an abiding presence, an unchanging deep stillness, an uncaused joy beyond good and bad. This is the joy of Being, the peace of God.

On the level of form, there is birth and death, creation and destruction, growth and dissolution, of seemingly separate forms. This is reflected everywhere: in the life cycle of a star or a planet, a physical body, a tree, a flower; in the rise and fall of nations, political systems, civilizations; and in the inevitable cycles of gain and loss in the life of an individual.

There are cycles of success, when things come to you and thrive, and cycles of failure, when they wither or disintegrate and you have to let them go in order to make room for new things to arise, or for transformation to happen. If you cling and resist at that point, it means you are refusing to go with the flow of life, and you will suffer.

It is not true that the up cycle is good and the down cycle bad, except in the mind's judgment. Growth is usually considered positive, but nothing can grow forever. If growth, of whatever kind, were to go on and on, it would eventually become monstrous and destructive. Dissolution is needed for new growth to happen. One cannot exist without the other.

The down cycle is absolutely essential for spiritual realization. You must have failed deeply on some level or experienced some deep loss or pain to be drawn to the spiritual dimension. Or perhaps your very success became empty and meaningless and so turned out to be failure. Failure lies concealed in every success, and success in every failure. In this world, which is to say on the level of form, everybody "fails" sooner or later, of course, and every achievement eventually comes to naught. All forms are impermanent.

You can still be active and enjoy manifesting and creating new forms and circumstances, but you won't be identified with them. You do not need them to give you a sense of self. They are not your life — only your life situation.

Your physical energy is also subject to cycles. It cannot always be at a peak. There will be times of low as well as high energy. There will be periods when you are highly active and creative, but there may also be times when everything seems stagnant, when it seems that you are not getting anywhere, not achieving anything. A cycle can last for anything from a few hours to a few years. There are large cycles and small cycles within these large ones. Many illnesses are created through fighting against the cycles of low energy, which are vital for regeneration. The compulsion to do, and the tendency to derive your sense of self-worth and identity from external factors such as achievement, is an inevitable illusion as long as you are identified with the mind. This makes it hard or impossible for you to accept the low cycles and allow them to be. Thus, the intelligence of the organism may take over as a self-protective measure and create an illness in order to force you to stop, so that the necessary regeneration can take place.

The cyclical nature of the universe is closely linked with the impermanence of all things and situations. The Buddha made this a central part of his teaching. All conditions are highly unstable and in constant flux, or, as he put it, impermanence is a characteristic of every condition, every situation you will ever encounter in your life. It will change, disappear, or no longer satisfy you. Impermanence is also central to Jesus's teaching: "Do not lay up for yourselves treasures on earth, where moth and rust consume and where thieves break in and steal...."

As long as a condition is judged as "good" by your mind, whether it be a relationship, a possession, a social role, a place, or your physical body, the mind attaches itself to it and identifies with it. It makes you happy, makes you feel good about yourself, and it may become part of who you are or think you are. But nothing lasts in this dimension where moth and rust consume. Either it ends or it changes, or it may undergo a polarity shift: The same condition that was good yesterday or last year has suddenly or gradually turned into bad. The same condition that made you happy, then makes you unhappy. The prosperity of today becomes the empty consumerism of tomorrow. The happy wedding and honeymoon become the unhappy divorce or the unhappy coexistence. Or a condition disappears, so its absence makes you unhappy. When a condition or situation that the mind has attached itself to and identified with changes or disappears, the mind cannot accept it. It will cling to the disappearing condition and resist the change. It is almost as if a limb were being torn off your body.

We sometimes hear of people who have lost all their money or whose reputation has been ruined committing suicide. Those are the extreme cases. Others, whenever a major loss of one kind or another occurs, just become deeply unhappy or make themselves ill. They cannot distinguish between their life and their life situation. I recently read about a famous actress who died in her eighties. As her beauty started to fade and became ravaged by old age, she grew desperately unhappy and became a recluse. She, too, had identified with a condition: her external appearance. First, the condition gave her a happy sense of self, then an unhappy one. If she had been able to connect with the formless and timeless life within, she could have watched and allowed the fading of her external form from a place of serenity and peace. Moreover, her external form would have become increasingly transparent to the light shining through from her ageless true nature, so her beauty would not really have faded but simply become transformed into spiritual beauty. However, nobody told her that this is possible. The most essential kind of knowledge is not yet widely accessible.

The Buddha taught that even your happiness is *dukkha* — a Pali word meaning "suffering" or "unsatisfactoriness." It is inseparable from its opposite. This means that your happiness and unhappiness are in fact one. Only the illusion of time separates them.

This is not being negative. It is simply recognizing the nature of things, so that you don't pursue an illusion for the rest of your life.

Nor is it saying that you should no longer appreciate pleasant or beautiful things or conditions. But to seek something through them that they cannot give — an identity, a sense of permanency and fulfillment — is a recipe for frustration and suffering. The whole advertising industry and consumer society would collapse if people became enlightened and no longer sought to find their identity through *things*. The more you seek happiness in this way, the more it will elude you. Nothing out there will ever satisfy you except temporarily and superficially, but you may need to experience many disillusionments before you realize that truth. Things and conditions can give you pleasure, but they will also give you pain. Things and conditions can give you pleasure, but they cannot give you *joy*. Nothing can *give* you joy. Joy is uncaused and arises from within as the joy of Being. It is an essential part of the inner state of peace, the state that has been called the peace of God. It is your natural state, not something that you need to work hard for or struggle to attain.

Many people never realize that there can be no "salvation" in anything they do, possess, or attain. Those who do realize it often become world-weary and depressed: if nothing can give you true fulfillment, what is there left to strive for, what is the point in anything? The Old Testament prophet must have arrived at such a realization when he wrote "I have seen everything that is done under the sun, and behold, all is vanity and a striving after wind." When you reach this point, you are one step away from despair — and one step away from enlightenment.

A Buddhist monk once told me: "All I have learned in the twenty years that I have been a monk I can sum up in one sentence: All that arises passes away. This I know." What he meant, of course, was this: I have learned to offer no resistance to what *is*; I have learned to allow the present moment to be and to accept the impermanent nature of all things and conditions. Thus have I found peace.

To offer no resistance to life is to be in a state of grace, ease, and lightness. This state is then no longer dependent upon things being in a certain way, good or bad. It seems almost paradoxical, yet when your inner dependency on form is gone, the general conditions of your life, the outer forms, tend to improve greatly. Things, people, or conditions that you thought you needed for your happiness now come to you with no struggle or effort on your part, and you are free to enjoy and appreciate them — while they last. All those things, of course, will still pass away, cycles will come and go, but with dependency gone there is no fear of loss anymore. Life flows with ease.

The happiness that is derived from some secondary source is never very deep. It is only a pale reflection of the joy of Being, the vibrant peace that you find within as you enter the state of nonresistance. Being takes you beyond the polar opposites of the mind and frees you from dependency on form. Even if everything were to collapse and crumble all around you, you would still feel a deep inner core of peace. You may not be happy, but you will be at peace.

USING AND RELINQUISHING NEGATIVITY

All inner resistance is experienced as negativity in one form or another. All negativity *is* resistance. In this context, the two words are almost synonymous. Negativity ranges from irritation or impatience to fierce anger, from a depressed mood or sullen resentment to suicidal despair. Sometimes the resistance triggers the emotional painbody, in which case even a minor situation may produce intense negativity, such as anger, depression, or deep grief.

The ego believes that through negativity it can manipulate reality and get what it wants. It believes that through it, it can attract a desirable condition or dissolve an undesirable one. *A Course in Miracles* rightly points out that, whenever you are unhappy, there is the unconscious belief that the unhappiness "buys" you what you want. If "you" — the mind — did not believe that unhappiness works, why would you create it? The fact is, of course, that negativity does not work. Instead of attracting a desirable condition, it stops it from arising. Instead of dissolving an undesirable one, it keeps it in place. Its only "useful" function is that it strengthens the ego, and that is why the ego loves it.

Once you have identified with some form of negativity, you do not want to let go, and on a deeply unconscious level, you do not want positive change. It would threaten your identity as a depressed, angry, or hard-done-by person. You will then ignore, deny or sabotage the positive in your life. This is a common phenomenon. It is also insane.

Negativity is totally unnatural. It is a psychic pollutant, and there is a deep link between the poisoning and destruction of nature and the vast negativity that has accumulated in the collective human psyche. No other life form on the planet knows negativity, only humans, just as no other life form violates and poisons the Earth that sustains it. Have you ever seen an unhappy flower or a stressed oak tree? Have you come across a depressed dolphin, a frog that has a problem with self-esteem, a cat that cannot relax, or a bird that carries hatred and resentment? The only animals that may occasionally experience something akin to negativity or show signs of neurotic behavior are those that live in close contact with humans and so link into the human mind and its insanity.

Watch any plant or animal and let it teach you acceptance of what *is*, surrender to the Now. Let it teach you Being. Let it teach you integrity — which means to be one, to be yourself, to be real. Let it teach you how to live and how to die, and how *not* to make living and dying into a problem.

I have lived with several Zen masters — all of them cats. Even ducks have taught me important spiritual lessons. Just watching them is a meditation. How peacefully they float along, at ease with themselves, totally present in the Now, dignified and perfect as only a mindless creature can be. Occasionally, however, two ducks will get into a fight — sometimes for no apparent reason, or because one duck has strayed into another's private space. The fight usually lasts only for a few seconds, and then the ducks separate, swim off in opposite directions, and vigorously flap their wings a few times. They then continue to swim on peacefully as if the fight had never happened. When I observed that for the first time, I suddenly realized that by flapping their wings they were releasing surplus energy, thus preventing it from becoming trapped in their body and turning into negativity. This is natural wisdom, and it is easy for them because they do not have a mind that keeps the past alive unnecessarily and then builds an identity around it.

Couldn't a negative emotion also contain an important message? For example, if I often feel depressed, it may be a signal that there is something wrong with my life, and it may force me to look at my life situation and make some changes. So I need to listen to what the emotion is telling me and not just dismiss it as negative.

Yes, recurring negative emotions do sometimes contain a message, as do illnesses. But any changes that you make, whether they have to do with your work, your relationships, or your surroundings, are ultimately only cosmetic unless they arise out of a change in your level of consciousness. And as far as that is concerned, it can only mean one thing: becoming more present. When you have reached a certain degree of presence, you don't need negativity anymore to tell you what is needed in your life situation. But as long as negativity *is* there, use it. Use it as a kind of signal that reminds you to be more present.

How do we stop negativity from arising, and how do we get rid of it once it is there?

As I said, you stop it from arising by being fully present. But don't become discouraged. There are as yet few people on the planet who can sustain a state of continuous presence, although some are getting close to it. Soon, I believe, there will be many more.

Whenever you notice that some form of negativity has arisen within you, look on it not as a failure, but as a helpful signal that is telling you: "Wake up. Get out of your mind. Be present."

There is a novel by Aldous Huxley called *Island*, written in his later years when he became very interested in spiritual teachings. It tells the story of a man shipwrecked on a remote island cut off from the rest of the world. This island contains a unique civilization. The unusual thing about it is that its inhabitants, unlike those of the rest of the world, are actually sane. The first thing that the man notices are the colorful parrots perched in the trees, and they seem to be constantly croaking the words "Attention. Here and Now. Attention. Here and Now." We later learn that the islanders taught them these words in order to be reminded continuously to stay present.

So whenever you feel negativity arising within you, whether caused by an external factor, a thought, or even nothing in particular that you are aware of, look on it as a voice saying "Attention. Here and Now. Wake up." Even the slightest irritation is significant and needs to be acknowledged and looked at; otherwise, there will be a cumulative build-up of unobserved reactions. As I said before, you may be able to just drop it once you realize that you don't want to have this energy field inside you and that it serves no purpose. But then make sure that you drop it completely. If you cannot drop it, just accept that it is there and take your attention into the feeling, as I pointed out earlier.

As an alternative to dropping a negative reaction, you can make it disappear by imagining yourself becoming transparent to the external cause of the reaction. I recommend that you practice it with little, even trivial, things first. Let's say that you are sitting quietly at home. Suddenly, there is the penetrating sound of a car alarm from across the street. Irritation arises. What is the purpose of the irritation? None whatsoever. Why did you create it? You didn't. The mind did. It was totally automatic, totally unconscious. Why did the mind create it? Because it holds the unconscious belief that its resistance, which you experience as negativity or unhappiness in some form, will

159

somehow dissolve the undesirable condition. This, of course, is a delusion. The resistance that it creates, the irritation or anger in this case, is far more disturbing than the original cause that it is attempting to dissolve.

All this can be transformed into spiritual practice. Feel yourself becoming transparent, as it were, without the solidity of a material body. Now allow the noise, or whatever causes a negative reaction, to pass right through you. It is no longer hitting a solid "wall" inside you. As I said, practice with little things first. The car alarm, the dog barking, the children screaming, the traffic jam. Instead of having a wall of resistance inside you that gets constantly and painfully hit by things that "should not be happening," let everything pass through you.

Somebody says something to you that is rude or designed to hurt. Instead of going into unconscious reaction and negativity, such as attack, defense, or withdrawal, you let it pass right through you. Offer no resistance. It is as if there is nobody there to get hurt anymore. *That* is forgiveness. In this way, you become invulnerable. You can still tell that person that his or her behavior is unacceptable, if that is what you choose to do. But that person no longer has the power to control your inner state. You are then in your power — not in someone else's, nor are you run by your mind. Whether it is a car alarm, a rude person, a flood, an earthquake, or the loss of all your possessions, the resistance mechanism is the same.

I have been practicing meditation, I have been to workshops, I have read many books on spirituality, I try to be in a state of nonresistance — but if you ask me whether I have found true and lasting inner peace, my honest answer would have to be "no." Why haven't I found it? What else can I do?

You are still seeking outside, and you cannot get out of the seeking mode. Maybe the next workshop will have the answer, maybe that new technique. To you I would say: Don't look for peace. Don't look for any other state than the one you are in now; otherwise, you will set up inner conflict and unconscious resistance. Forgive yourself for not being at peace. The moment you *completely* accept your non-peace, your non-peace becomes transmuted into peace. Anything you accept fully will get you there, will take you into peace. This is the miracle of surrender.

∫

You may have heard the phrase "turn the other cheek," which a great teacher of enlightenment used 2,000 years ago. He was attempting to convey symbolically the secret of nonresistance and nonreaction. In this statement, as in all his others, he was concerned only with your inner reality, not with the outer conduct of your life.

Do you know the story of Banzan? Before he became a great Zen master, he spent many years in the pursuit of enlightenment, but it eluded him. Then one day, as he was walking in the marketplace, he overheard a conversation between a butcher and his customer. "Give me the best piece of meat you have," said the customer. And the butcher replied, "Every piece of meat I have is the best. There is no piece of meat here that is not the best." Upon hearing this, Banzan became enlightened.

I can see you are waiting for some explanation. When you accept what *is*, every piece of meat — every moment — is the best. That is enlightenment.

THE NATURE OF COMPASSION

Having gone beyond the mind-made opposites, you become like a deep lake. The outer situation of your life and whatever happens there, is the surface of the lake. Sometimes calm, sometimes windy and rough, according to the cycles and seasons. Deep down, however, the lake is always undisturbed. You are the whole lake, not just the surface, and you are in touch with your own depth, which remains absolutely still. You don't resist change by mentally clinging to any situation. Your inner peace does not depend on it. You abide in Being — unchanging, timeless, deathless — and you are no longer dependent for fulfillment or happiness on the outer world of constantly fluctuating forms. You can enjoy them, play with them, create new forms, appreciate the beauty of it all. But there will be no need to attach yourself to any of it.

When you become this detached, does it not mean that you also become remote from other human beings?

On the contrary. As long as you are unaware of Being, the reality of other humans will elude you, because you have not found your own. Your mind will like or dislike their form, which is not just their body but includes their mind as well. True relationship becomes possible only when there is an awareness of Being. Coming from Being, you will perceive another person's body and mind as just a screen, as it were, behind which you can feel their true reality, as you feel yours. So, when confronted with someone else's suffering or unconscious behavior, you stay present and in touch with Being and are thus able to look beyond the form and feel the other person's radiant and pure Being through your own. At the level of Being, all suffering is recognized as an illusion. Suffering is due to identification with form. Miracles of healing sometimes occur through this realization, by awakening Being-consciousness in others — if they are ready.

Is that what compassion is?

Yes. Compassion is the awareness of a deep bond between yourself and all creatures. But there are two sides to compassion, two sides to this bond. On the one hand, since you are still here as a physical body, you share the vulnerability and mortality of your physical form with every other human and with every living being. Next time you say "I

162

have nothing in common with this person," remember that you have a great deal in common: A few years from now — two years or seventy years, it doesn't make much difference — both of you will have become rotting corpses, then piles of dust, then nothing at all. This is a sobering and humbling realization that leaves little room for pride. Is this a negative thought? No, it is a fact. Why close your eyes to it? In that sense, there is total equality between you and every other creature.

One of the most powerful spiritual practices is to meditate deeply on the mortality of physical forms, including your own. This is called: Die before you die. Go into it deeply. Your physical form is dissolving, is no more. Then a moment comes when all mind-forms or thoughts also die. Yet *you* are still there — the divine presence that you are. Radiant, fully awake. Nothing that was real ever died, only names, forms, and illusions.

The realization of this deathless dimension, your true nature, is the other side of compassion. On a deep feeling-level, you now recognize not only your own immortality but through your own that of every other creature as well. On the level of form, you share mortality and the precariousness of existence. On the level of Being, you share eternal, radiant life. These are the two aspects of compassion. In compassion, the seemingly opposite feelings of sadness and joy merge into one and become transmuted into a deep inner peace. This is the peace of God. It is one of the most noble feelings that humans are capable of, and it has great healing and transformative power. But true compassion, as I have just described it, is as yet rare. To have deep empathy for the suffering of another being certainly requires a high degree of consciousness but represents only one side of compassion. It is not complete. True compassion goes beyond empathy or sympathy. It does not happen until sadness merges with joy, the joy of Being beyond form, the joy of eternal life.

TOWARD A DIFFERENT ORDER OF REALITY

I don't agree that the body needs to die. I am convinced that we can achieve physical immortality. We believe in death and that's why the body dies.

The body does not die because you believe in death. The body exists, or seems to, because you believe in death. Body and death are part of the same illusion, created by the egoic mode of consciousness, which has no awareness of the Source of life and sees itself as separate and constantly under threat. So it creates the illusion that you are a body, a dense, physical vehicle that is constantly under threat.

To perceive yourself as a vulnerable body that was born and a little later dies — that's the illusion. Body and death: one illusion. You cannot have one without the other. You want to keep one side of the illusion and get rid of the other, but that is impossible. Either you keep all of it or you relinquish all of it.

However, you cannot escape from the body, nor do you have to. The body is an incredible misperception of your true nature. But your true nature is concealed somewhere within that illusion, not outside it, so the body is still the only point of access to it.

If you saw an angel but mistook it for a stone statue, all you would have to do is adjust your vision and look more closely at the "stone statue," not start looking somewhere else. You would then find that there never was a stone statue.

If belief in death creates the body, why does an animal have a body? An animal doesn't have an ego, and it doesn't believe in death....

But it still dies, or seems to.

Remember that your perception of the world is a reflection of your state of consciousness. You are not separate from it, and there is no objective world out there. Every moment, your consciousness creates the world that you inhabit. One of the greatest insights that has come out of modern physics is that of the unity between the observer and the observed: the person conducting the experiment — the observing consciousness — cannot be separated from the observed phenomena, and a different way of looking causes the observed phenomena to behave differently. If you believe, on a deep level, in separation and the struggle for survival, then you see that belief reflected all around you and your perceptions are governed by fear. You inhabit a world of death and of bodies fighting, killing, and devouring each other.

Nothing is what it seems to be. The world that you create and see through the egoic mind may seem a very imperfect place, even a vale of tears. But whatever you perceive is only a kind of symbol, like an image in a dream. It is how your consciousness interprets and interacts with the molecular energy dance of the universe. This energy is the raw material of so-called physical reality. You see it in terms of bodies and birth and death, or as a struggle for survival. An infinite number of completely different interpretations, completely different worlds, is possible and, in fact, exists — all depending on the perceiving consciousness. Every being is a focal point of consciousness, and every such focal point creates its own world, although all those worlds are interconnected. There is a human world, an ant world, a dolphin world, and so on. There are countless beings whose consciousness frequency is so different from yours that you are probably unaware of their existence, as they are of yours. Highly conscious beings who are aware of their connectedness with the Source and with each other would inhabit a world that to you would appear as a heavenly realm — and yet all worlds are ultimately one.

Our collective human world is largely created through the level of consciousness we call mind. Even within the collective human world there are vast differences, many different "sub-worlds," depending on the perceivers or creators of their respective worlds. Since all worlds are interconnected, when collective human consciousness becomes transformed, nature and the animal kingdom will reflect that transformation. Hence the statement in the Bible that in the coming age "The lion shall lie down with the lamb." This points to the possibility of a completely different order of reality.

The world as it appears to us now is, as I said, largely a reflection of the egoic mind. Fear being an unavoidable consequence of egoic delusion, it is a world dominated by fear. Just as the images in a dream are symbols of inner states and feelings, so our collective reality is largely a symbolic expression of fear and of the heavy layers of negativity that have accumulated in the collective human psyche. We are not separate from our world, so when the majority of humans become free of egoic delusion, this inner change will affect all of creation. You will literally inhabit a new world. It is a shift in planetary consciousness. The strange Buddhist saying that every tree and every blade of grass will eventually become enlightened points to the same truth. According to St. Paul, the whole of creation is waiting for humans to become enlightened. That is how I interpret his saying that "The created universe is waiting with eager expectation for God's sons to be revealed." St. Paul goes on to say that all of creation will become redeemed through this: "Up to the present...the whole created universe in all its parts groans as if in the pangs of childbirth."

What is being born is a new consciousness and, as its inevitable reflection, a new world. This is also foretold in the New Testament Book of Revelation: "Then I saw a new heaven and a new earth, for the first heaven and the first earth had passed away."

But don't confuse cause and effect. Your primary task is not to seek salvation through creating a better world, but to awaken out of identification with form. You are then no longer bound to this world, this level of reality. You can feel your roots in the Unmanifested and so are free of attachment to the manifested world. You can still enjoy the passing pleasures of this world, but there is no fear of loss anymore, so you don't need to cling to them. Although you can enjoy sensory pleasures, the craving for sensory experience is gone, as is the constant search for fulfillment through psychological gratification, through feeding the ego. You are in touch with something infinitely greater than any pleasure, greater than any manifested thing.

In a way, you then don't need the world anymore. You don't even need it to be different from the way it is.

It is only at this point that you begin to make a real contribution toward bringing about a better world, toward creating a different order of reality. It is only at this point that you are able to feel true compassion and to help others at the level of cause. Only those who have transcended the world can bring about a better world.

You may remember that we talked about the dual nature of true compassion, which is awareness of a common bond of shared mortality and immortality. At this deep level, compassion becomes healing in the widest sense. In that state, your healing influence is primarily based not on doing but on being. Everybody you come in contact with will be touched by your presence and affected by the peace that you emanate, whether they are conscious of it or not. When you are fully present and people around you manifest unconscious behavior, you won't feel the need to react to it, so you don't give it any reality. Your peace is so vast and deep that anything that is not peace disappears into it as if it had never existed. This breaks the karmic cycle of action and reaction. Animals, trees, flowers will feel your peace and respond to it. You teach through being, through demonstrating the peace of God. You become the "light of the world," an emanation of pure consciousness, and so you eliminate suffering on the level of cause. You eliminate unconsciousness from the world.

This doesn't mean that you may not also teach through doing — for example, by pointing out how to disidentify from the mind, recognize unconscious patterns within oneself, and so on. But who you *are* is

167

always a more vital teaching and a more powerful transformer of the world than what you say, and more essential even than what you do. Furthermore, to recognize the primacy of Being, and thus work on the level of cause, does not exclude the possibility that your compassion may simultaneously manifest on the level of doing and of effect, by alleviating suffering whenever you come across it. When a hungry person asks you for bread and you have some, you will give it. But as you give the bread, even though your interaction may only be very brief, what really matters is this moment of shared Being, of which the bread is only a symbol. A deep healing takes place within it. In that moment, there is no giver, no receiver.

But there shouldn't be any hunger and starvation in the first place. How can we create a better world without tackling evils such as hunger and violence first?

All evils are the *effect* of unconsciousness. You can alleviate the effects of unconsciousness, but you cannot eliminate them unless you eliminate their cause. True change happens within, not without.

If you feel called upon to alleviate suffering in the world, that is a very noble thing to do, but remember not to focus exclusively on the outer; otherwise, you will encounter frustration and despair. Without a profound change in human consciousness, the world's suffering is a bottomless pit. So don't let your compassion become one-sided. Empathy with someone else's pain or lack and a desire to help need to be balanced with a deeper realization of the eternal nature of all life and the ultimate illusion of all pain. Then let your peace flow into whatever you do and you will be working on the levels of effect and cause simultaneously.

This also applies if you are supporting a movement designed to stop deeply unconscious humans from destroying themselves, each other, and the planet, or from continuing to inflict dreadful suffering on other sentient beings. Remember: Just as you cannot fight the darkness, so you cannot fight unconsciousness. If you try to do so, the polar opposites will become strengthened and more deeply entrenched. You will become identified with one of the polarities, you will create an "enemy," and so be drawn into unconsciousness yourself. Raise awareness by disseminating information, or at the most, practice passive resistance. But make sure that you carry no resistance within, no hatred, no negativity. "Love your enemies," said Jesus, which, of course, means "have no enemies."

Once you get involved in working on the level of effect, it is all too easy to lose yourself in it. Stay alert and very, very present. The causal level needs to remain your primary focus, the teaching of enlightenment your main purpose, and peace your most precious gift to the world.

CHAPTER TEN

THE MEANING OF SURRENDER

ACCEPTANCE OF THE NOW

You mentioned "surrender" a few times. I don't like that idea. It sounds somewhat fatalistic. If we always accept the way things are, we are not going to make any effort to improve them. It seems to me what progress is all about, both in our personal lives and collectively, is not to accept the limitations of the present but to strive to go beyond them and create something better. If we hadn't done this, we would still be living in caves. How do you reconcile surrender with changing things and getting things done?

To some people, surrender may have negative connotations, implying defeat, giving up, failing to rise to the challenges of life, becoming lethargic, and so on. True surrender, however, is something entirely different. It does not mean to passively put up with whatever situation you find yourself in and to do nothing about it. Nor does it mean to cease making plans or initiating positive action.

Surrender is the simple but profound wisdom of *yielding to* rather than *opposing* the flow of life. The only place where you can experience the flow of life is the Now, so to surrender is to accept the present moment unconditionally and without reservation. It is to relinquish inner resistance to what *is*. Inner resistance is to say "no" to what *is*, through mental judgment and emotional negativity. It becomes particularly pronounced when things "go wrong," which means that there is a gap between the demands or rigid expectations of your mind and what *is*. That is the pain gap. If you have lived long enough, you will know that things "go wrong" quite often. It is precisely at those times that surrender needs to be practiced if you want to eliminate pain and sorrow from your life. Acceptance of what *is* immediately frees you from mind identification and thus reconnects you with Being. Resistance *is* the mind.

Surrender is a purely inner phenomenon. It does not mean that on the outer level you cannot take action and change the situation. In fact, it is not the overall situation that you need to accept when you surrender, but just the tiny segment called the Now.

For example, if you were stuck in the mud somewhere, you wouldn't say: "Okay, I resign myself to being stuck in the mud." Resignation is not surrender. You don't need to accept an undesirable or unpleasant life situation. Nor do you need to deceive yourself and say that there is nothing wrong with being stuck in the mud. No. You recognize fully that you want to get out of it. You then narrow your attention down to the present moment without mentally labeling it in any way. This means that there is no judgment of the Now. Therefore, there is no resistance, no emotional negativity. You accept the "isness" of this moment. Then you take action and do all that you can to get out of the mud. Such action I call positive action. It is far more effective than negative action, which arises out of anger, despair, or frustration. Until you achieve the desired result, you continue to practice surrender by refraining from labeling the Now.

Let me give you a visual analogy to illustrate the point I am making. You are walking along a path at night, surrounded by a thick fog. But you have a powerful flashlight that cuts through the fog and creates a narrow, clear space in front of you. The fog is your life situation, which includes past and future; the flashlight is your conscious presence; the clear space is the Now.

Non-surrender hardens your psychological form, the shell of the ego, and so creates a strong sense of separateness. The world around you and people in particular come to be perceived as threatening. The unconscious compulsion to destroy others through judgment arises, as does the need to compete and dominate. Even nature becomes your enemy and your perceptions and interpretations are governed by fear. The mental disease that we call paranoia is only a slightly more acute form of this normal but dysfunctional state of consciousness.

Not only your psychological form but also your physical form — your body — becomes hard and rigid through resistance. Tension arises in different parts of the body, and the body as a whole contracts. The free flow of life energy through the body, which is essential for its healthy functioning, is greatly restricted. Bodywork and certain forms of physical therapy can be helpful in restoring this flow, but unless you practice surrender in your everyday life, those things can only give temporary symptom relief since the cause — the resistance pattern — has not been dissolved.

There is something within you that remains unaffected by the transient circumstances that make up your life situation, and only through surrender do you have access to it. It is your life, your very Being — which exists eternally in the timeless realm of the present. Finding this life is "the one thing that is needed" that Jesus talked about.

If you find your life situation unsatisfactory or even intolerable, it is only by surrendering first that you can break the unconscious resistance pattern that perpetuates that situation.

Surrender is perfectly compatible with taking action, initiating change or achieving goals. But in the surrendered state a totally different energy, a different quality, flows into your doing. Surrender reconnects you with the source-energy of Being, and if your doing is infused with Being, it becomes a joyful celebration of life energy that takes you more deeply into the Now. Through nonresistance, the quality of your consciousness and, therefore, the quality of whatever you are doing or creating is enhanced immeasurably. The results will then look after themselves and reflect that quality. We could call this "surrendered action." It is not work as we have known it for thousands of years. As more humans awaken, the word *work* is going to disappear from our vocabulary, and perhaps a new word will be created to replace it.

It is the quality of your consciousness at this moment that is the main determinant of what kind of future you will experience, so to surrender is the most important thing you can do to bring about positive change. Any action you take is secondary. No truly positive action can arise out of an unsurrendered state of consciousness.

I can see that if I am in a situation that is unpleasant or unsatisfactory and I completely accept the moment as it is, there will be no suffering or unhappiness. I will have risen above it. But I still can't quite see where the energy or motivation for taking action and bringing about change would come from if there isn't a certain amount of dissatisfaction.

In the state of surrender, you see very clearly what needs to be done, and you take action, doing one thing at a time and focusing on one thing at a time. Learn from nature: See how everything gets accomplished and how the miracle of life unfolds without dissatisfaction or unhappiness. That's why Jesus said: "Look at the lilies, how they grow; they neither toil nor spin."

If your overall situation is unsatisfactory or unpleasant, *separate out this instant* and surrender to what *is*. That's the flashlight cutting through the fog. Your state of consciousness then ceases to be controlled by external conditions. You are no longer coming from reaction and resistance.

Then look at the specifics of the situation. Ask yourself, "Is there anything I can do to change the situation, improve it, or remove myself from it?" If so, you take appropriate action. Focus not on the 100 things that you will or may have to do at some future time but on the one thing that you can do now. This doesn't mean you should not do any planning. It may well be that planning is the one thing you can do now. But make sure you don't start to run "mental movies," project yourself into the future, and so lose the Now. Any action you take may not bear fruit immediately. Until it does — do not resist what is. If there is no action you can take, and you cannot remove yourself from the situation either, then use the situation to make you go more deeply into surrender, more deeply into the Now, more deeply into Being. When you enter this timeless dimension of the present, change often comes about in strange ways without the need for a great deal of doing on your part. Life becomes helpful and cooperative. If inner factors such as fear, guilt, or inertia prevented you from taking action, they will dissolve in the light of your conscious presence.

Do not confuse surrender with an attitude of "I can't be bothered anymore" or "I just don't care anymore." If you look at it closely, you will find that such an attitude is tainted with negativity in the form of hidden resentment and so is not surrender at all but masked resistance. As you surrender, direct your attention inward to check if there is any trace of resistance left inside you. Be very alert when you do so; otherwise, a pocket of resistance may continue to hide in some dark corner in the form of a thought or an unacknowledged emotion.

FROM MIND ENERGY TO SPIRITUAL ENERGY

Letting go of resistance is easier said than done. I still don't see clearly how to let go. If you say it is by surrendering, the question remains: "How?"

Start by acknowledging that there *is* resistance. *Be* there when it happens, when the resistance arises. Observe how your mind creates it, how it labels the situation, yourself, or others. Look at the thought process involved. Feel the energy of the emotion. By witnessing the resistance, you will see that it serves no purpose. By focusing all your attention on the Now, the unconscious resistance is made conscious, and that is the end of it. You cannot be conscious *and* unhappy, conscious *and* in negativity. Negativity, unhappiness, or suffering in whatever form means that there is resistance, and resistance is always unconscious.

Surely I can be conscious of my unhappy feelings?

Would you choose unhappiness? If you did not choose it, how did it arise? What is its purpose? Who is keeping it alive? You say that you are conscious of your unhappy feelings, but the truth is that you are identified with them and keep the process alive through compulsive thinking. All *that* is unconscious. If you were conscious, that is to say totally present in the Now, all negativity would dissolve almost instantly. It could not survive in your presence. It can only survive in your absence. Even the pain-body cannot survive for long in your presence. You keep your unhappiness alive by giving it time. That is its lifeblood. Remove time through intense present-moment awareness and it dies. But do you want it to die? Have you truly had enough? Who would you be without it?

Until you practice surrender, the spiritual dimension is something you read about, talk about, get excited about, write books about, think about, believe in — or don't, as the case may be. It makes no difference. Not until you surrender does it become a living reality in your life. When you do, the energy that you emanate and which then runs your life is of a much higher vibrational frequency than the mind energy that still runs our world — the energy that created the existing social, political, and economic structures of our civilization, and which also continuously perpetuates itself through our educational systems and the media. Through surrender, spiritual energy comes into this world. It creates no suffering for yourself, for other humans, or any other life form on the planet. Unlike mind energy, it does not pollute the earth, and it is not subject to the law of polarities, which dictates that nothing can exist without its opposite, that there can be no good without bad. Those who run on mind energy, which is still the vast majority of the Earth's population, remain unaware of the existence of spiritual energy. It belongs to a different order of reality and will create a different world when a sufficient number of humans enter the surrendered state and so become totally free of negativity. If the Earth is to survive, this will be the energy of those who inhabit it.

Jesus referred to this energy when he made his famous prophetic statement in the Sermon on the Mount: "Blessed are the gentle; they shall have the earth for their possession." It is a silent but intense presence that dissolves the unconscious patterns of the mind. They may still remain active for a while, but they won't run your life anymore. The external conditions that were being resisted also tend to shift or dissolve quickly through surrender. It is a powerful transformer of situations and people. If conditions do not shift immediately, your acceptance of the Now enables you to rise above them. Either way, you are free.

SURRENDER IN PERSONAL RELATIONSHIPS

What about people who want to use me, manipulate or control me? Am I to surrender to them?

They are cut off from Being, so they unconsciously attempt to get energy and power from you. It is true that only an unconscious person will try to use or manipulate others, but it is equally true that only an unconscious person *can* be used and manipulated. If you resist or fight unconscious behavior in others, you become unconscious yourself. But surrender doesn't mean that you allow yourself to be used by unconscious people. Not at all. It is perfectly possible to say "no" firmly and clearly to a person or to walk away from a situation and be in a state of complete inner nonresistance at the same time. When you say "no" to a person or a situation, let it come not from reaction but from insight, from a clear realization of what is right or not right for you at that moment. Let it be a nonreactive "no," a high-quality "no," a "no" that is free of all negativity and so creates no further suffering.

I am in a situation at work that is unpleasant. I have tried to surrender to it, but I find it impossible. A lot of resistance keeps coming up.

If you cannot surrender, take action immediately: Speak up or do something to bring about a change in the situation — or remove yourself from it. Take responsibility for your life. Do not pollute your beautiful, radiant inner Being nor the Earth with negativity. Do not give unhappiness in any form whatsoever a dwelling place inside you.

If you cannot take action, for example if you are in prison, then you have two choices left: resistance or surrender. Bondage or inner freedom from external conditions. Suffering or inner peace.

Is nonresistance also to be practiced in the external conduct of our lives, such as nonresistance to violence, or is it something that just concerns our inner life?

You only need to be concerned with the inner aspect. That is primary. Of course, that will also transform the conduct of your outer life, your relationships, and so on.

Your relationships will be changed profoundly by surrender. If you can never accept what *is*, by implication you will not be able to accept anybody the way they are. You will judge, criticize, label, reject, or attempt to change people. Furthermore, if you continuously make the Now into a means to an end in the future, you will also make every person you encounter or relate with into a means to an end. The relationship — the human being — is then of secondary importance to you, or of no importance at all. What you can get out of the relationship is primary — be it material gain, a sense of power, physical pleasure, or some form of ego gratification.

Let me illustrate how surrender can work in relationships. When you become involved in an argument or some conflict situation, perhaps with a partner or someone close to you, start by observing how defensive you become as your own position is attacked, or feel the force of your own aggression as you attack the other person's

THE MEANING OF SURRENDER

position. Observe the attachment to your views and opinions. Feel the mental-emotional energy behind your need to be right and make the other person wrong. That's the energy of the egoic mind. You make it conscious by acknowledging it, by feeling it as fully as possible. Then one day, in the middle of an argument, you will suddenly realize that you have a choice, and you may decide to drop your own reaction — just to see what happens. You surrender. I don't mean dropping the reaction just verbally by saying "Okay, you are right," with a look on your face that says, "I am above all this childish unconsciousness." That's just displacing the resistance to another level, with the egoic mind still in charge, claiming superiority. I am speaking of letting go of the entire mental-emotional energy field inside you that was fighting for power.

The ego is cunning, so you have to be very alert, very present, and totally honest with yourself to see whether you have truly relinquished your identification with a mental position and so freed yourself from your mind. If you suddenly feel very light, clear and deeply at peace, that is an unmistakable sign that you have truly surrendered. Then observe what happens to the other person's mental position as you no longer energize it through resistance. When identification with mental positions is out of the way, true communication begins.

What about nonresistance in the face of violence, aggression, and the like?

Nonresistance doesn't necessarily mean doing nothing. All it means is that any "doing" becomes nonreactive. Remember the deep wisdom underlying the practice of Eastern martial arts: don't resist the opponent's force. Yield to overcome.

Having said that, "doing nothing" when you are in a state of intense presence is a very powerful transformer and healer of situations and people. In Taoism, there is a term called *wu wei*, which is usually translated as "actionless activity" or "sitting quietly doing nothing." In ancient China, this was regarded as one of the highest achievements or virtues. It is radically different from inactivity in the ordinary state of consciousness, or rather unconsciousness, which stems from fear, inertia, or indecision. The real "doing nothing" implies inner nonresistance and intense alertness.

On the other hand, if action is required, you will no longer react from your conditioned mind, but you will respond to the situation out of your conscious presence. In that state, your mind is free of concepts, including the concept of nonviolence. So who can predict what you will do?

The ego believes that in your resistance lies your strength, whereas in truth resistance cuts you off from Being, the only place of true power. Resistance is weakness and fear masquerading as strength. What the ego sees as weakness is your Being in its purity, innocence, and power. What it sees as strength is weakness. So the ego exists in a continuous resistance-mode and plays counterfeit roles to cover up your "weakness," which in truth is your power.

Until there is surrender, unconscious role-playing constitutes a large part of human interaction. In surrender, you no longer need ego defenses and false masks. You become very simple, very real. "That's dangerous," says the ego. "You'll get hurt. You'll become vulnerable." What the ego doesn't know, of course, is that only through the letting go of resistance, through becoming "vulnerable," can you discover your true and essential invulnerability.

TRANSFORMING ILLNESS INTO ENLIGHTENMENT

If someone is seriously ill and completely accepts their condition and surrenders to the illness, would they not have given up their will to get back to health? The determination to fight the illness would not be there any more, would it?

Surrender is inner acceptance of what *is* without any reservations. We are talking about your *life* — this instant — not the conditions or circumstances of your life, not what I call your life situation. We have spoken about this already.

With regard to illness, this is what it means. Illness is part of your life situation. As such, it has a past and a future. Past and future form an uninterrupted continuum, unless the redeeming power of the Now is activated through your conscious presence. As you know, underneath the various conditions that make up your life situation, which exists in time, there is something deeper, more essential: your Life, your very Being in the timeless Now.

As there are no problems in the Now, there is no illness either. The belief in a label that someone attaches to your condition keeps the condition in place, empowers it, and makes a seemingly solid reality out of a temporary imbalance. It gives it not only reality and solidity but also a continuity in time that it did not have before. By focusing on this instant and refraining from labeling it mentally, illness is reduced to one or several of these factors: physical pain, weakness, discomfort, or disability. *That* is what you surrender to — now. You do not surrender to the idea of "illness." Allow the suffering to force you into the present moment, into a state of intense conscious presence. Use it for enlightenment.

Surrender does not transform what *is*, at least not directly. Surrender transforms *you*. When *you* are transformed, your whole world is transformed, because the world is only a reflection. We spoke about this earlier.

If you looked in the mirror and did not like what you saw, you would have to be mad to attack the image in the mirror. That is precisely what you do when you are in a state of nonacceptance. And, of course, if you attack the image, it attacks you back. If you accept the image, no matter what it is, if you become friendly toward it, it cannot *not* become friendly toward you. This is how you change the world.

Illness is not the problem. *You* are the problem — as long as the egoic mind is in control. When you are ill or disabled, do not feel that you have failed in some way, do not feel guilty. Do not blame life for treating you unfairly, but do not blame yourself either. All that is resistance. If you have a major illness, use it for enlightenment.

Anything "bad" that happens in your life — use it for enlightenment. Withdraw time from the illness. Do not give it any past or future. Let it force you into intense present-moment awareness — and see what happens.

Become an alchemist. Transmute base metal into gold, suffering into consciousness, disaster into enlightenment.

Are you seriously ill and feeling angry now about what I have just said? Then that is a clear sign that the illness has become part of your sense of self and that you are now protecting your identity — as well as protecting the illness. The condition that is labeled "illness" has nothing to do with who you truly are.

WHEN DISASTER STRIKES

As far as the still unconscious majority of the population is concerned, only a critical limit-situation has the potential to crack the hard shell of the ego and force them into surrender and so into the awakened state. A limit-situation arises when through some disaster, drastic upheaval, deep loss, or suffering your whole world is shattered and doesn't make sense anymore. It is an encounter with death, be it physical or psychological. The egoic mind, the creator of this world, collapses. Out of the ashes of the old world, a new world can then come into being.

There is no guarantee, of course, that even a limit-situation will do it, but the potential is always there. Some people's resistance to what *is* even intensifies in such a situation, and so it becomes a descent into hell. In others, there may only be partial surrender, but even that will give them a certain depth and serenity that were not there before. Parts of the ego shell break off, and this allows small amounts of the radiance and peace that lie beyond the mind to shine through.

Limit-situations have produced many miracles. There have been murderers in death row waiting for execution who, in the last few hours of their lives, experienced the egoless state and the deep joy and peace that come with it. The inner resistance to the situation they

found themselves in became so intense as to produce unbearable suffering, and there was nowhere to run and nothing to do to escape it,
not even a mind-projected future. So they were forced into complete
acceptance of the unacceptable. They were forced into surrender. In
this way, they were able to enter the state of grace with which comes
redemption: complete release from the past. Of course, it is not really the limit-situation that makes room for the miracle of grace and
redemption but the act of surrender.

So whenever any kind of disaster strikes, or something goes seriously "wrong" — illness, disability, loss of home or fortune or of a
socially defined identity, break-up of a close relationship, death or suffering of a loved one, or your own impending death — know that there
is another side to it, that you are just one step away from something
incredible: a complete alchemical transmutation of the base metal of
pain and suffering into gold. That one step is called surrender.

I do not mean to say that you will become happy in such a situation. You will not. But fear and pain will become transmuted into an
inner peace and serenity that come from a very deep place — from
the Unmanifested itself. It is "the peace of God, which passes all
understanding." Compared to that, happiness is quite a shallow
thing. With this radiant peace comes the realization — not on the
level of mind but within the depth of your Being — that you are indestructible, immortal. This is not a belief. It is absolute certainty that
needs no external evidence or proof from some secondary source.

TRANSFORMING SUFFERING INTO PEACE

*I read about a stoic philosopher in ancient Greece who, when he was
told that his son had died in an accident, replied, "I knew he was not
immortal." Is that surrender? If it is, I don't want it. There are some
situations in which surrender seems unnatural and inhuman.*

Being cut off from your feelings is not surrender. But we don't know
what his inner state was when he said those words. In certain
extreme situations, it may still be impossible for you to accept the

Now. But you always get a second chance at surrender.

Your first chance is to surrender each moment to the reality of that moment. Knowing that what *is* cannot be undone — because it already *is* — you say yes to what *is* or accept what isn't. Then you do what you have to do, whatever the situation requires. If you abide in this state of acceptance, you create no more negativity, no more suffering, no more unhappiness. You then live in a state of nonresistance, a state of grace and lightness, free of struggle.

Whenever you are unable to do that, whenever you miss that chance — either because you are not generating enough conscious presence to prevent some habitual and unconscious resistance pattern from arising, or because the condition is so extreme as to be absolutely unacceptable to you — then you are creating some form of pain, some form of suffering. It may look as if the situation is creating the suffering, but ultimately this is not so — your resistance is.

Now here is your second chance at surrender: If you cannot accept what is outside, then accept what is *inside*. If you cannot accept the external condition, accept the internal condition. This means: Do not resist the pain. Allow it to be there. Surrender to the grief, despair, fear, loneliness, or whatever form the suffering takes. Witness it without labeling it mentally. Embrace it. Then see how the miracle of surrender transmutes deep suffering into deep peace. This is your crucifixion. Let it become your resurrection and ascension.

I do not see how one can surrender to suffering. As you yourself pointed out, suffering is non-surrender. How could you surrender to nonsurrender?

Forget about surrender for a moment. When your pain is deep, all talk of surrender will probably seem futile and meaningless anyway. When your pain is deep, you will likely have a strong urge to escape from it rather than surrender to it. You don't want to feel what you feel. What could be more normal? But there is no escape, no way out. There are many pseudo escapes — work, drink, drugs, anger, projection, suppression, and so on — but they don't free you from the pain. Suffering does not diminish in intensity when you make it unconscious. When you deny emotional pain, everything you do or think as well as your relationships become contaminated with it. You broadcast it, so to speak, as the energy you emanate, and others will pick it up subliminally. If they are unconscious, they may even feel compelled to attack or hurt you in some way, or you may hurt them in an unconscious projection of your pain. You attract and manifest whatever corresponds to your inner state.

When there is no way out, there is still always a way *through*. So don't turn away from the pain. Face it. Feel it fully. *Feel* it — don't *think* about it! Express it if necessary, but don't create a script in your mind around it. Give all your attention to the feeling, not to the person, event, or situation that seems to have caused it. Don't let the mind use the pain to create a victim identity for yourself out of it. Feeling sorry for yourself and telling others your story will keep you stuck in suffering. Since it is impossible to get away from the feeling, the only possibility of change is to move into it; otherwise, nothing will shift. So give your complete attention to what you feel, and refrain from mentally labeling it. As you go into the feeling, be intensely alert. At first, it may seem like a dark and terrifying place, and when the urge to turn away from it comes, observe it but don't act on it. Keep putting your attention on the pain, keep feeling the grief, the fear, the dread, the loneliness, whatever it is. Stay alert, stay present — present with your whole Being, with every cell of your body. As you do so, you are bringing a light into this darkness. This is the flame of your consciousness.

At this stage, you don't need to be concerned with surrender anymore. It has happened already. How? Full attention *is* full acceptance, is surrender. By giving full attention, you use the power of the Now, which is the power of your presence. No hidden pocket of resistance can survive in it. Presence removes time. Without time, no suffering, no negativity, can survive.

The acceptance of suffering is a journey into death. Facing deep pain, allowing it to be, taking your attention into it, is to enter death consciously. When you have died this death, you realize that there is no death — and there is nothing to fear. Only the ego dies. Imagine a ray of sunlight that has forgotten it is an inseparable part of the sun and deludes itself into believing it has to fight for survival and create and cling to an identity other than the sun. Would the death of this delusion not be incredibly liberating?

Do you want an easy death? Would you rather die without pain, without agony? Then die to the past every moment, and let the light of your presence shine away the heavy, time-bound self you thought of as "you."

∫

THE WAY OF THE CROSS

There are many accounts of people who say they have found God through their deep suffering, and there is the Christian expression "the way of the cross," which I suppose points to the same thing.

We are concerned with nothing else here.

Strictly speaking, they did not find God through their suffering, because suffering implies resistance. They found God through surrender, through total acceptance of what *is*, into which they were forced by their intense suffering. They must have realized on some level that their pain was self-created.

How do you equate surrender with finding God?

Since resistance is inseparable from the mind, relinquishment of resistance — surrender — is the end of the mind as your master, the impostor pretending to be "you," the false god. All judgment and all

186

negativity dissolve. The realm of Being, which had been obscured by the mind, then opens up. Suddenly, a great stillness arises within you, an unfathomable sense of peace. And within that peace, there is great joy. And within that joy, there is love. And at the innermost core, there is the sacred, the immeasurable, That which cannot be named.

I don't call it finding God, because how can you find that which was never lost, the very life that you are? The word God is limiting not only because of thousands of years of misperception and misuse, but also because it implies an entity other than you. God is Being itself, not a being. There can be no subject-object relationship here, no duality, no you *and* God. God-realization is the most natural thing there is. The amazing and incomprehensible fact is not that you *can* become conscious of God but that you are *not* conscious of God.

The way of the cross that you mentioned is the old way to enlightenment, and until recently it was the only way. But don't dismiss it or underestimate its efficacy. It still works.

The way of the cross is a complete reversal. It means that the worst thing in your life, your cross, turns into the best thing that ever happened to you, by forcing you into surrender, into "death," forcing you to become as nothing, to become as God — because God, too, is no-thing.

At this time, as far as the unconscious majority of humans is concerned, the way of the cross is still the only way. They will only awaken through further suffering, and enlightenment as a collective phenomenon will be predictably preceded by vast upheavals. This process reflects the workings of certain universal laws that govern the growth of consciousness and thus was foreseen by some seers. It is described, among other places, in the Book of Revelation or Apocalypse, though cloaked in obscure and sometimes impenetrable symbology. This suffering is inflicted not by God but by humans on themselves and on each other as well as by certain defensive measures that the Earth, which is a living, intelligent organism, is going to take to protect herself from the onslaught of human madness.

However, there is a growing number of humans alive today whose consciousness is sufficiently evolved not to need any more suffering before the realization of enlightenment. You may be one of them.

Enlightenment through suffering — the way of the cross — means to be forced into the kingdom of heaven kicking and screaming. You finally surrender because you can't stand the pain anymore, but the pain could go on for a long time until this happens. Enlightenment consciously chosen means to relinquish your attachment to past and future and to make the Now the main focus of your life. It means choosing to dwell in the state of presence rather than in time. It means saying yes to what *is*. You then don't need pain anymore. How much more time do you think you will need before you are able to say "I will create no more pain, no more suffering?" How much more pain do you need before you can make that choice?

If you think that you need more time, you will get more time — and more pain. Time and pain are inseparable.

THE POWER TO CHOOSE

What about all those people who, it seems, actually want to suffer? I have a friend whose partner is physically abusive toward her, and her previous relationship was of a similar kind. Why does she choose such men, and why is she refusing to get out of that situation now? Why do so many people actually choose pain?

I know that the word *choose* is a favorite New Age term, but it isn't entirely accurate in this context. It is misleading to say that somebody "chose" a dysfunctional relationship or any other negative situation in his or her life. Choice implies consciousness — a high degree of consciousness. Without it, you have no choice. Choice begins the moment you disidentify from the mind and its conditioned patterns, the moment you become present. Until you reach that point, you are unconscious, spiritually speaking. This means that you are compelled to think, feel, and act in certain ways according to the conditioning of your mind. That is why Jesus said: "Forgive them, for they know not what they do." This is not related to intelligence in the conventional sense of the word. I have met many highly intelligent and educated people who were also completely unconscious, which is to say completely identified with their mind. In fact, if mental development and increased knowledge are not counterbalanced by a corresponding growth in consciousness, the potential for unhappiness and disaster is very great.

Your friend is stuck in a relationship with an abusive partner, and not for the first time. Why? No choice. The mind, conditioned as it is by the past, always seeks to re-create what it knows and is familiar with. Even if it is painful, at least it is familiar. The mind always adheres to the known. The unknown is dangerous because it has no control over it. That's why the mind dislikes and ignores the present moment. Present-moment awareness creates a gap not only in the stream of mind but also in the past-future continuum. Nothing truly new and creative can come into this world except through that gap, that clear space of infinite possibility.

So your friend, being identified with her mind, may be re-creating a pattern learned in the past in which intimacy and abuse are inseparably linked. Alternatively, she may be acting out a mind pattern learned in early childhood according to which she is unworthy and deserves to be punished. It is possible, too, that she lives a large part of her life through the pain-body, which always seeks more pain on which to feed. Her partner has his own unconscious patterns, which complement hers. Of course her situation is self-created, but who or what is the self that is doing the creating? A mental-emotional pattern from the past, no more. Why make a self out of it? If you tell her that she has chosen her condition or situation, you are reinforcing her state of mind identification. But is her mind pattern who she is? Is it her self? Is her true identity derived from the past? Show your friend how to be the observing presence behind her thoughts and her emotions. Tell her about the pain-body and how to free herself from it. Teach her the art of inner-body awareness. Demonstrate to her the meaning of presence. As soon as she is able to access the power of the Now, and thereby break through her conditioned past, she *will* have a choice.

Nobody *chooses* dysfunction, conflict, pain. Nobody *chooses* insanity. They happen because there is not enough presence in you to dissolve the past, not enough light to dispel the darkness. You are not fully here. You have not quite woken up yet. In the meantime, the conditioned mind is running your life.

Similarly, if you are one of the many people who have an issue with their parents, if you still harbor resentment about something they did or did not do, then you still believe that they had a choice — that they could have acted differently. It always *looks* as if people had a choice, but that is an illusion. As long as your mind with its conditioned patterns runs your life, as long as you *are* your mind, what choice do you have? None. You are not even there. The mind-identified state is severely dysfunctional. It is a form of insanity. Almost everyone is suffering from this illness in varying degrees. The moment you realize this, there can be no more resentment. How can you resent someone's illness? The only appropriate response is compassion.

So that means nobody is responsible for what they do? I don't like that idea.

If you are run by your mind, although you have no choice you will still suffer the consequences of your unconsciousness, and you will create further suffering. You will bear the burden of fear, conflict, problems, and pain. The suffering thus created will eventually force you out of your unconscious state.

What you say about choice also applies to forgiveness, I suppose. You need to be fully conscious and surrender before you can forgive.

"Forgiveness" is a term that has been in use for 2,000 years, but most people have a very limited view of what it means. You cannot truly forgive yourself or others as long as you derive your sense of self from the past. Only through accessing the power of the Now, which is your own power, can there be true forgiveness. This renders the past powerless, and you realize deeply that nothing you ever did or that was ever done to you could touch even in the slightest the radiant essence of who you are. The whole concept of forgiveness then becomes unnecessary.

And how do I get to that point of realization?

When you surrender to what *is* and so become fully present, the past ceases to have any power. You do not need it anymore. Presence is the key. The Now is the key.

How will I know when I have surrendered?

When you no longer need to ask the question.

NOTES

1. A. Koestler, *The Ghost in the Machine* (Arkana, London 1989), p. 180.

2. Z. Brzezinski, *The Grand Failure* (Charles Scribner's Sons, New York 1989), pp. 239-40.

3. *A Course in Miracles* (Foundation for Inner Peace, 1990), Introduction.

4. R. L. Sivard, *World Military and Social Expenditures 1996, 16th Edition* (World Priorities, Washington D.C., 1996), p. 7.

ABOUT THE AUTHOR

Eckhart Tolle was born in Germany, where he spent the first thirteen years of his life. After graduating from the University of London, he was a research scholar and supervisor at Cambridge University. When he was twenty-nine, a profound spiritual transformation virtually dissolved his old identity and radically changed the course of his life.

The next few years were devoted to understanding, integrating, and deepening that transformation, which marked the beginning of an intense inward journey.

Eckhart is not aligned with any particular religion or tradition. In his teaching, he conveys a simple yet profound message with the timeless and uncomplicated clarity of the ancient spiritual masters: there is a way out of suffering and into peace.

Eckhart is currently traveling extensively, taking his teachings and his presence throughout the world. He has lived in Vancouver, Canada, since 1996.

Eckhart Tolle in Mumbai, India, in February 2002.

For information on talks, satsangs, intensives, retreats, and
meditations given by Eckhart Tolle see:

www.eckharttolle.com

For further details contact:
Yogi Impressions Books Pvt. Ltd.
61, Anjali, Minoo Desai Road, Colaba,
Mumbai 400 005, India.
Website: www.yogiimpressions.com

Telephone: (022) 284-2923/4/6
Fax: (022) 204-6825
E-mail: yogi@yogiimpressions.com

Visit
www.indiayogi.com

India's leading spiritual portal.

If you wish to order more copies please use the following order form.

THE POWER OF NOW
A GUIDE TO SPIRITUAL ENLIGHTENMENT

ORDER BY

Telephone (022) 2842923/4/6 **Fax** (022) 2046825

E-mail yogi@yogiimpressions.com

Postal Orders

Yogi Impressions
61, Anjali, Minoo Desai Road,
Colaba, Mumbai 400 005, India.
Website: www.yogiimpressions.com

PRICE

Rs. 225/-

Shipping & handling (extra)

Mumbai: Rs. 25/- (courier) per book

Rest of India: Rs. 40/- (air courier) per book

MAIL TO

Name

Company Name (if applicable)

Address

City   Pin code   State

Telephone (   )   E-mail

NUMBER OF COPIES [   ] Note: 20% discount on single orders of 5 books or more

PAYMENT

☐ Cheque (Mumbai)   ☐ Cheque (Rest of India)   ☐ Pay Order   ☐ Demand Draft

Amount (inclusive of shipping and handling)

Signature   Date

• Payment to be made in favour of Yogi Impressions
• Please allow 2 weeks after clearance of payment for order processing and delivery
• When ordering 2 or more books please ensure you add Rs. 25 or Rs. 40 per book (as outlined above) for shipping & handling

ALSO PUBLISHED BY YOGI IMPRESSIONS

Practicing The Power Of Now
by Eckhart Tolle

In this handy companion book to his internationally best-selling 'The Power of Now' – Eckhart Tolle has extracted the essence of his spiritual teaching and arranged it with a set of meditations and exercises to actually help people lead a more liberated life.

Reflect on his words. Reflect even on the space between the words. And, maybe over time, maybe immediately – you will find the power and discover the path to "a life of grace, ease and lightness." It is all there in this handy companion book. And, it is now within your hands. Discover its power to change and elevate your everyday life.

Start practicing the power of 'Now'.

Size: 7¼" × 5", Paperback

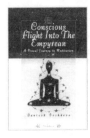

Conscious Flight Into The Empyrean
by Santosh Sachdeva

'Conscious Flight Into The Empyrean' is a touching revelation of a contemporary mystical experience and understanding.

This rare depiction of the visual unfolding of the Kundalini energy challenges conventional views of perception and experience. The book is a first-hand account of an extraordinary voyage into the subtle realms; with the author's own illustrations of the visions seen in her daily meditations.

The author practices meditation and experiences visions of pillars of light, stars encircling her form, and snakes twirling on top of her head. She travels through tunnels of light to zoom into the incredible experience of oneness with the universe.

Size: 9" × 6", Paperback, Art Paper, in color

The Money Tarot Book
by Rohit Arya

'The Money Tarot Book' does a clear and precise card-by-card analysis for you and helps you arrive at sound, swift and practical decision-making in matters related to your career, business and personal finance.

It does not require long periods of familiarization. It is extremely simple to use and does not need any specific Tarot pack to work with. Any pack will do.

'The Money Tarot Book' is not a substitute for decisive action on your part, but it helps you gain a wider perspective about the situation and provide some purpose and motivation. It will prove to be a significant source of advice and emotional strength in your financial decisions.

Size: 8¼" × 5", Paperback

A Simple Monk
Writings on His Holiness The Dalai Lama

Born to humble farmer-parents... Declared at the age of two years as the 14th Dalai Lama... Awarded the Nobel Peace Prize in 1992... This simple monk is today a statesman, diplomat, politician, beloved leader of an exiled people and, above all, a peacemaker for the world.

Replete with never-before published photographs by Alison Wright, it captures – through articles written by his mother Diki Tsering and renowned authors like Orville Schell, Pico Iyer, Spalding Grey and Prof. Robert A.F. Thurman – the multi-dimensional personality of His Holiness The Dalai Lama... a spiritual leader for the new millennium.

Size: 10$\frac{1}{4}$" × 10$\frac{1}{4}$", Hardbound, Art Paper, Full Color – Imported by Yogi Impressions Books through a special arrangement with New World Library, USA.

The Secret
by Áine Keenan

'The Secret' is a contemplation in verse on the nature of Identity, Reality and Mystery. It possesses an appeal which is timeless and universal, speaking on many levels simultaneously, while mirroring the urge to bypass tradition and ritual with the ultimate objective of direct experience.

Áine travelled to Mumbai, India, to be in the presence of the famous *Advaita* sage Ramesh Balsekar and absorb his teachings. Balsekar's philosophy is the acceptance of the absoluteness of Divine Will based on the non-duality of *Advaita Vedanta*. This is an inspiring collection of poems written during the time when Áine attended the morning satsang at Balsekar's residence.

Size: 5$\frac{1}{4}$" × 4", Pocketbook

The Ultimate Understanding
by Ramesh Balsekar

A book containing the complete essentials of the Hindu philosophy of *Advaita* or Non-duality, by a man who is recognized as one of the foremost contemporary Indian sages. Backed by the total conviction of the final understanding of a true Master, this treasure of *Advaita* is unrivalled in its unique conceptual expression of the highest Truth, delivered with fundamental wisdom, simplicity, and clarity. Balsekar elaborates his own concepts with those of his Guru, Nisargadatta Maharaj, the Buddha, Ramana Maharshi, Hindu scriptures, Taoist Masters and Wei Wu Wei, all serving as pointers to the Truth, to the ultimate understanding.

'The Ultimate Understanding' is perhaps the pinnacle of Balsekar's writing.

Size: 11¼" × 8¾", Hardbound, Art Paper